D0307751

# Battleground Europe

# WALKING THE SOMME

*Other guides in the Battleground Europe Series:*

**Somme - Serre** *by* Jack Horsfall & Nigel Cave
**Somme - Beaumont Hamel** *by* Nigel Cave
**Somme - Thiepval** *by* Michael Stedman
**Somme - La Boisselle** *by* Michael Stedman
**Ypres - Sanctuary Wood & Hooge** *by* Nigel Cave
**Arras - Vimy Ridge** *by* Nigel Cave
**The Hindenburg Line** *by* Peter Oldham

*Battleground Europe Series guides in preparation:*

**Somme - Fricourt**
**Somme - Carnoy-Montauban**
**Somme - Courcelette**
**Somme - Gommecourt**
**Somme - Delville Wood**
**Somme - Pozières**
**Ypres - Passchendaele**
**Ypres - Hill 60**

The last two decades have seen an enormous increase in the numbers of visitors to the battlefields and other sites of the Western Front, that area of France and Flanders which bore the brunt of fighting during the First World War. Sadly, until now the guide books available to the visitors - whether the casual tourist, the serious historian, or someone seeking the grave of, or memorial to, a relation - have generally been of poor quality and even poorer content, often merely adding to a reader's confusion. The **Battleground Europe series** of guides adopts a fresh approach, providing up-to-date information about sites, routes and other details, and taking the reader on a tour of the area covered by the book. Amply supplied with illustrations and maps, each volume contains a general history as well as covering a number of actions within the area, enabling today's observer to transform the impression from one of a rural scene to one of the horrors and heroism that characterised events during the Great War. The text directs readers to certain areas and operations, allowing them to visualise what they would have seen more than seventy years ago, and incorporates those pieces of evidence, whether trench or other surviving relic, cemetery, memorial or museum, that remain today as reminders of what happened so many years ago. Each author has been selected not only for his knowledge of the area and what happened there between 1914 and 1918, but also for his knowledge of the area as it is now, making these guides indispensable for the tourist and serious scholar alike.

# Battleground Europe

# WALKING THE SOMME

## A Walker's Guide to the 1916 Somme Battlefields

*Best wishes from the author,*

### Paul Reed

*[signature]*

*Lega Truss
Jul '99*

*Series editor*
**Nigel Cave**

**LEO COOPER**
London

This book is dedicated to the memory of:
**John Giles**
1921-1991
Author and Founder of the Western Front Association

*and to his wife*
**Margery Giles**

First published in 1997 by
LEO COOPER
190 Shaftesbury Avenue, London WC2H 8JL
an imprint of
Pen Sword Books Limited
47 Church Street, Barnsley, South Yorkshire S70 2AS

Copyright © Paul Reed, 1997

**ISBN 0 85052 567 5**

A CIP catalogue of this book is available
from the British Library

Printed by Redwood Books Limited
Trowbridge, Wiltshire

*For up-to-date information on other titles produced under the Leo
Cooper imprint, please telephone or write to:*

Pen & Sword Books Ltd, FREEPOST, 47 Church Street
Barnsley, South Yorkshire S70 2AS
Telephone 01226 734222

# CONTENTS

Preface ..................................................................... 6
Users Guide .......................................................... 8
Bibliography .......................................................... 11

**Gommecourt** 1st July 1916 ................................. 13
**The Pals Walk** – Serre .................................... 29
**Beaumont-Hamel** ......................................... 46
**Ancre Valley** ................................................ 67
**Thiepval** ...................................................... 83
**The AIF** – Pozières Battlefield Walk .............. 103
**The Yorkshire Walk**: Fricourt 1st July 1916 .... 116
**The Poets' Walk**: Bois Francais and Mametz ..... 127
**Montauban** 1st July 1916 ............................. 139
**Behind the Lines** ........................................ 149
**The Dawn Attack**: Longueval 14th July 1916 .... 163
**High Wood** .................................................. 174
**The Tank Walk**: Longueval-Ginchy-Flers ......... 184
**Butte de Warlencourt** .................................. 194
**Guillemont Road** ......................................... 203

Abbreviations ...................................................... 213
Endnotes ............................................................ 215
Acknowledgements .............................................. 217
Index ................................................................. 219

# Preface

Why write this book? With so many guides to almost every corner of the Western Front... why another? But yet, despite the fact that many of these guides have been fine volumes in their own right, few have ever given the visitor to France a clear lead in actually walking the ground. At first I found this curious; the men in those times walked everywhere- often incredible distances. Then surely the only way to see the ground they fought over was to walk it too?

In my many years of visiting the Old Front Line, in a lifetime as short as the men who were there in those fateful years, I have seen few walking companions. Indeed, on my very first visit to the Somme, and in the height of August, I saw no-one; in those days the battlefields had become what Charles Douie had feared,

"... the time must come when travellers are
seen no more, and only the forest of graves
above the Ancre will remain to tell the tale
of that island race whose sons once were lords
of these woods and fields." [1]

I vowed that this would never be so. Books on the Great War were even then difficult to find, and I took inspiration from authors like John Giles, Rose Coombes and Martin Middlebrook whose books became my bibles. And then a veritable explosion of publications on the war, and in particular the Somme, meant that almost every corner of the battlefield was covered by some volume.

Each year I came to France again and again, and slowly built a band of brothers who came with me – or I with them – to a point where I was along the Old Front Line almost every month. Surely something must come of it? And something did; a desire to share with a much wider public than my friends the knowledge that would take them on foot across the fields and along the lanes which their grandfathers had known so well.

The Somme was the perfect place for walking – and remains so. Little has changed in and around Albert since it was rebuilt in the 1920s. The land is rolling, and similar in texture to the Sussex Downs, where I grew up. Large fields are cut by dusty tracks in summer, and muddy lanes in winter. Birdsong is everywhere; the beauty of this place often belies the tragedy that unfolded here in 1916.

And so this book. A starting point for, I hope, pilgrims old and new. Wherever possible I have tried to include new information about the battle sites, cemeteries and individual graves. Some of them mentioned here I have seen a hundred times, and felt they, too, needed to be known by more visitors. Remembrance is a personal thing, and in some of the larger cemeteries it is often impossible to imagine anything but numbers; I hope that here a few faces are put to the splash of white stone found in the beautiful soldier cemeteries of the Somme.

And so to the walking. Much of the research for this book was done between May and August of 1994; long days, beautiful blue skies – 1st July weather, as one fellow pilgrim I met out there put it. I took great enjoyment from walking these routes, often on my own, sometimes with friends; and I only hope the reader and pilgrim will take equal pleasure. Sometimes, out on the road near Serre, or on the high ground at Hawthorn Ridge – or was it the valley in front of High Wood? – I often chanced the faint echo of footsteps following along behind... the 'lords of these woods and fields' are with us still, I at least, would earnestly like to believe.

Paul Reed
*Sussex & The Somme*
*Summer 1996*

**Men of the East Yorkshire Regiment on the march to the front line.**

# User Guide

THE WALKS: The scope of this book is aimed at the most common form of traveller to the Somme; individuals or small groups in a car. Each walk is circular, so that a vehicle can be left in a given location, and returned to (usually) without having to walk back across the same route. However, the walks will suit anyone visiting the battlefields in coach parties, by foot alone, or bicycle or mountain bike.

DURATION: The length of the walks are shown in hours (or part of) in each case, to give some idea of how much walking is required. This is based on a gentle stroll, taking time to stop and look at the surroundings, and discuss the areas you visit.

THE MAPS: The maps are based on field sketches drawn by the author during the research for this book. They have been re-drawn and made true-to-scale wherever possible. All maps have been simplified and usually only show roads, tracks and other features directly connected with the walk in question. They are, however, suitable for orientation purposes.

GETTING THERE: The Somme is one of the most accessible areas of the Western Front to reach. By car it is only an hour and a half on the Autoroute (motorway) from Calais. The area can be reached by train (and ferry) from London via Amiens or Arras. One operator currently (1996) runs an inexpensive overnight coach service from London to Amiens. Details of French railways can be obtained from the French Railways (SNCF) office in London. Cars can be hired in Amiens, and bikes in Albert.

ACCOMMODATION: There are many places to stay on the Somme; from Hotels in Albert, to Gites in villages, camp sites and Bed and Breakfast establishments. Many of the latter are increasingly being run by British families who have moved out to the Somme permanently. They offer good value, and a friendly welcome if you are unsure of Continental ways. However, Picardy people remain amongst the most friendly and unassuming in France. Further details of accommodation can be found in the Visitors' Centre at Delville Wood and in the Syndicat d'Initiative, opposite the Basilica in Albert. The French Tourist Office in London may be able to help with more general accommodation enquiries.

WHAT TO TAKE: As always with Northern France, the weather can be mixed and waterproofs, a spare jumper and strong shoes are never wasted on a trip to the battlefields. In the Summer, extra water, sun lotion and a hat are equally useful. Good walking boots are recommended for all walkers. Although there are many inexpensive models currently on the market, the more money you spend on a pair of boots, the longer they are likely to last. Ones that are already, or easily made, waterproof are essential. A small walker's rucksack is useful for carrying supplies, camera and other gear; again a waterproofed one would be a wise choice.

**The Iron Harvest: the result of one ploughing near Guillemont, February 1996.**

THE IRON HARVEST: Each year ploughing on the Somme battlefields unearths a vast arsenal of live ammunition, shells, grenades and mortar bombs. All should be regarded as dangerous and not touched under any circumstances. Even over eighty years later these deadly relics cause casualties. Safe souvenirs can be bought at Delville Wood and in the Musee des Abris in Albert.

WESTERN FRONT ASSOCIATION: For those with more than a passing interest in the Great War membership of the WFA is essential. One years subscription includes three copies of both *Stand To!* (the WFA's glossy magazine) and the *Bulletin* (the in-house newsletter). There are dozens of local branches throughout the UK and abroad. It is good for making useful contacts, exchanging information and ideas, and the only place to buy copies of original trench maps. For further information contact:

> The Western Front Association
> PO BOX 1914
> Reading
> Berkshire
> RG4 7YP

NOTE: The author and publishers bear no responsibility for any events or injuries which arise through the walking of these routes, nor the interpretation or misinterpretation of any directions or maps. All walks are conducted at the walkers own risk and responsibility.

**Gordon Highlanders on the way up to the front overtake a wounded German prisoner on a wheeled stretcher.**

# Bibliography

At the end of every walk is a short reading list with books specifically relating to the subject of that walk. Other useful books include:

## General

Bean, C.E.W.     *Official History of Australia in the War of 1914-18* Vol 3 (no publisher 1929)
Christie, N.     *For King & Empire: The Canadians on the Somme- A Social History and Battlefield Tour* (CEF Books 1996)
Coombs, R.E.B.   *Before Endeavours Fade* (After The Battle new edn 1994)
Giles, J.        *The Somme Then & Now* (After The Battle 1986)
Gliddon, G.      *When The Barrage Lifts* (Gliddon Books 1987)
Gliddon, G.      *VCs of the Somme- A Biographical Portrait* (Gliddon Books 1991)
Holt, T. & V.    *Major & Mrs Holt's Battlefield Guide To The Somme* (Pen & Sword 1996)
Hurst, S.C.      *The Silent Cities* (Methuen 1929)
James, E.A.      *British Regiments 1914-18* (Samson Books 1978)
Laffin, J.       *Australian Battlefields of the Western Front* (Kangaroo Press 1992)
Liddle, P.       *The Soldier's War 1914-1918* (Blandford Press 1988)
Liddle, P.       *The 1916 Battle of the Somme: A Reappraisal* (Leo Cooper 1992)
McCarthy, C.     *The Somme: The Day-by-Day Account* (Arms & Armour Press 1993)
MacDonald, L.    *Somme* (Michael Joseph 1983)
Middlebrook, M.  *The First Day on the Somme* (Allen Lane 1971)
Middlebrook, M.  *The Somme Battlefields* (Viking 1991)
Parsons, W.D.    *Pilgrimage: A Guide to the Royal Newfoundland Regiment in World War One* (Creative Publishers 1994)
Powell, A.       *A Deep Cry: First World War Soldier Poets* (Palladour Books 1993)
Roberts, C.G.D.  *Canada In Flanders Vol 3* (Hodder and Stoughton 1918)
Simkins, P.      *Kitchener's Army* (Manchester University Press 1988)
Simkins, P.      *World War 1 : 1914-1918 : The Western Front* (Tiger Books 1994)
Westlake, R.     *Kitchener's Army* (Nutshell Publishing 1989)
Westlake, R.     *British Battalions on the Somme* (Leo Cooper 1994)

## Additional Recommended Memoirs etc

Buckley, F.      *Q.6.A and Other Places* (Spottiswoode 1920)
Chapman, G.      *A Passionate Prodigality* (MacGibbon & Kee 1965)
Congreve, B.     *Armageddon Road: A VC's Diary* (Kimber 1982)
Dunn, J.C.       *The War The Infantry Knew 1914-1919* (1938)
Feilding, R.     *War Letters to a Wife* (Medici 1929)

11

| | |
|---|---|
| Glubb, J. | *Into Battle* (Cassell 1978) |
| Griffith, W. | *Up to Mametz* (Faber & Faber 1931) |
| Hitchcock, F.C. | *Stand To! A Diary of the Trenches 1915-18* (1937) |
| Hutchison, G.S. | *Footslogger* (Hutchinson 1931) |
| Hutchison, G.S. | *Pilgrimage* (Rich & Cowan 1935) |
| Hutchison, G.S. | *Warrior* (Hutchinson 1932) |
| Junger, E. | *Storm of Steel* (Chatto & Windus 1929) |
| Manning, F. | *Her Privates We* (Peter Davies 1930) |
| Masefield, J. | *The Old Front Line* (Heinemann 1917) |
| Pollard, A.O. | *Fire-Eater: The Memoirs of a V.C.* (Hutchinson n.d.) |
| Rogerson, S. | *Twelve Days* (Barker 1933) |
| Scott, F.G. | *The Great War As I Saw It* (Goodchild 1922) |
| Taylor, H.A. | *Goodbye to the Battlefields* (Paul 1928) |
| Tucker, J.F. | *Johnny Get Your Gun* (Kimber 1978) |
| Williamson, H. | *The Golden Virgin* (Macdonald 1957) |
| Williamson, H. | *The Wet Flanders Plain* (Faber & Faber 1929) |

**Waves of infantry walking over the battlefield near Ginchy during the battle of Morval. They are passing one of the four Mk 1 tanks detailed to lead the attack but which became unserviceable soon after zero hour.**

# GOMMECOURT 1ST JULY 1916 WALK

STARTING POINT: **Hebuterne Military Cemetery, Hebuterne**
DURATION: **4 hours**
WALK SUMMARY: **Starting from Hebuterne, the walk covers the ground over which the 56th (London) Division fought on 1st July 1916; moving on towards Foncquevillers, the 46th (North Midland) Division attack area is also examined.**

*Park your vehicle outside Hebuterne Military Cemetery, which is reached via a tree-lined lane running north from the D.27 Hebuterne-Sailly road.*

## HEBUTERNE MILITARY CEMETERY

The cemetery was started by units of the 48th (South Midland) Division in July 1915, when that division was one of the first to arrive on the Somme front. Hebuterne was then a village only a few hundred yards behind the front line, and heavily fortified. Despite its close proximity to the trenches, the village was in a good state of repair and remained this way until the opening of the 1916 Somme battle. Field Ambulances set up Advance Dressing Stations in Hebuterne, and began to use the cemetery for casualties who died of wounds. Due to being so close to the line, men killed in the forward trenches were often brought

**Hebuterne Military Cemetery in 1919.**     *Julian Sykes*

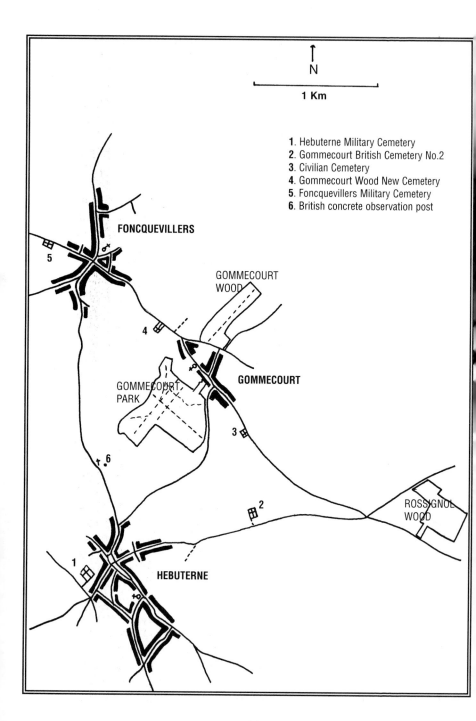

N

1 Km

1. Hebuterne Military Cemetery
2. Gommecourt British Cemetery No.2
3. Civilian Cemetery
4. Gommecourt Wood New Cemetery
5. Foncquevillers Military Cemetery
6. British concrete observation post

FONCQUEVILLERS

5

GOMMECOURT
WOOD

4

GOMMECOURT
PARK

GOMMECOURT

3

6

2

ROSSIGNOL
WOOD

1

HEBUTERNE

back here for burial. Plot I, Rows A-E, contain many of these early graves from the 48th Division period. The 48th was a territorial division, and in 1915 these 'Saturday Night Soldiers' had a bad reputation among many Army Commanders. The inscription on the grave of Lieutenant P.D. Doyne of the 1/4th Oxfs & Bucks Light Infantry (I-D-9) proudly claims what many of these territorials felt and were later to prove, 'we are able'.

The 56th (London) Division was another territorial unit that came to Hebuterne. The division had formed in March 1916 from some of the premier battalions of the London Regiment which had previously been scattered amongst a number of different formations. They held the sector from this time up to and beyond their attack on Gommecourt on 1st July 1916. Many London battalions secured particular areas of Hebuterne Military Cemetery to bury their dead, and as the structure of the cemetery has not changed since 1916 these regimental plots remain. For example, a large number of London Scottish burials can be found in Plot III, Rows G-H. Among them is Sergeant A.G. Morris (III-G-9), who died on 15th June 1916. The inscription on his stone additionally commemorates his brother, '... in memory of Second Lieutenant R.M. Morris Royal Fusiliers died 17.2.17 who lies near here'. This Morris, also a former member of the London Scottish, was killed at Boom Ravine, some distance away at Grandcourt, and has no known grave; his name can be found on the Thiepval Memorial. A London Regiment 1st July mass burial is in Plot IV, Row M, and reflects many of the units that lost heavily in the Gommecourt fighting.

Return to the entrance of the cemetery, **turn left** down the tree-lined lane and at the end **turn left** on the D.27 (Rue de Sailly) into the centre of Hebuterne. This road comes out into the main square of Hebuterne. During the war this was known as Shell Green as movement across it often attracted shell fire from German guns the other side of Gommecourt. The houses here all had cellars, so life went underground and whole battalions were billeted below the village. Towards the end of the square, where the village pond once stood, the distinctive Hebuterne  church is visible; a fair copy of the original which was destroyed in 1916.

From the main road junction in the square go **straight across** down Rue de Bucquoy, following the green CWGC signs for Gommecourt No.2 Cemetery, and passing the pleasant Cafe des Sports on the right hand corner. Follow this road to the outskirts of the village to a point where the road turns to the right. Stop just past a row of trees on the left. From here there is a fairly good view towards the distant trees of Gommecourt Park. The original pre-1916 front line ran in the fields on

**Hebuterne village and church under French occupation in 1915.**

the left to the park; just prior to 1st July it was extended to shorten the distance the 56th Division had to cross No Man's Land in the forthcoming attack. The 56th Division's role in the operations at Gommecourt was largely regarded as a sacrificial one; together with the 46th Division on their left, they were to attack Gommecourt to bite off

**Men of the London Scottish on their way to the fighting at Gommecourt, June 1916.**

the Gommecourt salient, and also to attract away as many German reserves as was possible from the major operations around Serre and beyond. The plan made no provision for any success in the fighting, and there were no reserves available to exploit any gains by either division. No attempt was made to hide or disguise the preparations for the attack; indeed British commanders went out of their way to make the build-up of troops, supplies and ammunition as obvious as possible, hopefully to make the Germans believe the major offensive would be against Gommecourt.

The operations here on 1st July were the responsibility of Lieutenant-General Snow's VII Corps, itself part of Allenby's Third Army. On the 56th Division front two full brigades were committed to the attack, with one in reserve at Hebuterne. The plan was to fight through the German trenches south of the village – all with names beginning with F – and circle round to the rear of Gommecourt to meet up with the 46th Division attacking on the left. The village could then be taken from the rear and new lines established east of Gommecourt. A full-sized model of the battlefield was constructed for training purposes at Sus-St-Leger, and all troops briefed as to their role in the attack.

**Continue along the road**. As you come out of the sunken part reached further along, stop and look again to the left for a good view towards Gommecourt. This position is just behind the new front line used in the 1st July operations. This was the attack area of 169 Brigade; on the far left near the Hebuterne-Gommecourt road the London Rifle

**9.2 inch Howitzers of the 96th Siege Battery RGA bombarding the Gommecourt trenches prior to 1st July attack.** *Malcolm Vyvyan*

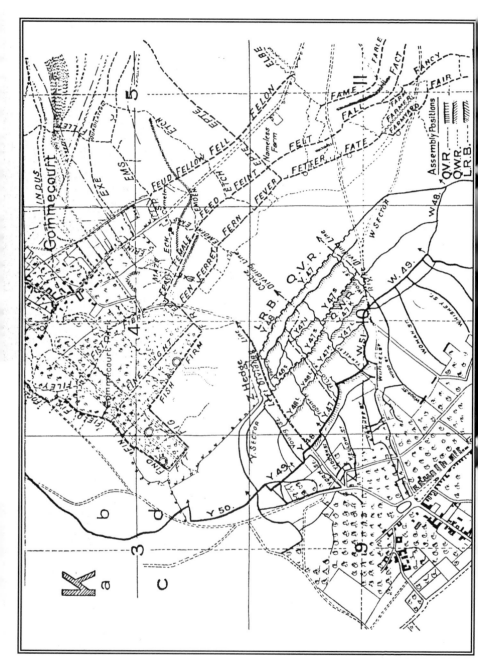

**Gommecourt trench map showing the dispositions for 56th (London) Division on 1st July 1916.**

Brigade (LRB) were in the first wave. To their right the Queen Victoria's Rifles (QVR) went over and crossing the road on which you are now standing the 12th Londons (Rangers) made their attack. Following up the QVRs were the Queen's Westminster Rifles (QWR). They moved forward from positions north of the sunken road you have just come through at zero hour – 7.30am – and advanced with the rest of the brigade into the valley visible to your left. Rifleman Aubrey Rose, a pre-war member of the QWRs, was a runner in the attack:

> 'We went over the top and eventually arrived in the German trenches. The smoke barrage was so thick you could not see where you were going and we didn't know it was a trap. They had withdrawn all their troops from the front line and left only a few. Many of these were either dead or dying. They had deep dug-outs and had set traps in them... the first dug-out our chaps went down had these German helmets [Picklehaube] which they thought would do nicely as souvenirs. But as they touched them they were blown up. The word soon got round after that; when we came to a dug-out, we didn't ask who was down there – it was just "Take that Fritz!" with a hand grenade.'[1]

**Rfn Aubrey Rose of the Queen's Westminster Rifles, England 1914.**

Rose's battalion, along with others in 169 Brigade, had done well. Within two hours they had taken all their objectives in and around Gommecourt. While preparing to move to the left to meet up with the 46th Division they encountered a large force of German reinforcements; the 46th Division had been cut down in No Man's Land on the left and were not – and never would be – coming. The resistance to this German counter-attack in the German third line was now reaching fever pitch. Aubrey Rose was there:

> '... eventually we landed in the German third line trenches. It was here I saw my company officer killed, Captain Mott. He'd been hit with his batman at the side of him. I had gone away on a message and when I came back both had gone; blown to pieces. I had the job afterwards of going to his parents to tell them what happened.
> The only officer left now was the bombing officer, and he was wounded. We were getting surrounded... our left

**Captain Hugh Fenwick Mott MC, KIA at Gommecourt 1st July 1916**
*Aubrey Rose*

flank was left open and the officer asked for volunteers to go back for reinforcements. I didn't volunteer because I was brave, but because I saw it as a chance to get back to our own trenches. So I went back into No Man's Land, it was then that the shock of seeing my officer killed got to me. I dropped to my knees and burst into tears.[2]

As the shells began to fall with even greater intensity, Aubrey Rose soon picked himself up and got back to the British lines. His call for reinforcements was passed on, but the barrage was so bad in No Man's Land by this time that no more troops could be brought up. The survivors of 168 and 169 Brigades had been forced back by counter-attacks into the old German front line, and after a further brutal attack just before dusk, the remaining Londoners were pushed back into No Man's Land and a general withdrawal to the British front line was made.

The attack on Gommecourt had cost the 56th Division a total of 183 officers and 4,131 other ranks. The Rangers alone, who attacked in the ground directly in front of you, lost over 450 men. Aubrey Rose's Queen's Westminsters had over 500 casualties; Rose became one of them. As he was making his way back through the Hebuterne communication trenches a German shrapnel shell wounded him in the back; he was eventually discharged and survived the war. The 56th Division's historian ended his account of the day's fighting on an optimistic note:

'The men of London had done well, although the salient remained in the hands of the enemy... there is no doubt that the main objective of the attack had been fulfilled. Unpleasant as it may seem, the role of the 56th Division was to induce the enemy to shoot at them with as many guns as could be gathered together.'[3]

Visible ahead is Gommecourt British Military Cemetery No.2; **continue along the road** to the cemetery. As you get nearer to it, the valley that was No Man's Land is clearly seen on the left.

## GOMMECOURT BRITISH CEMETERY NO.2

Gommecourt never fell to British troops during the Battle of the Somme, and was only taken when the Germans gave it up in the retreat to the Hindenburg Line in February 1917. After that date burial details cleared the Gommecourt battlefield, finding large concentrations of men who fell in the area on 1st July 1916. These were buried in four numbered Gommecourt cemeteries; Number 1, and Numbers 3 and 4, were in turn closed and concentrated into Gommecourt British

**The Valley before Gommecourt Park in 1919**
*Julian Sykes*

Cemetery No.2. Graves from the original No.2 Cemetery are now in Plot I; all 101 of them are men from the 56th Division units who died on 1st July. The other six plots contain 1,222 graves moved in not only from Gommecourt but from all the northern part of the Somme battlefield. In total there are 1,284 British graves, forty-six New Zealand, twenty-six Australian, and thirty-three special memorials; of these 681 graves are unknown. Every unit in 168 and 169 Brigades is represented in this cemetery; among them two brothers (III-B-12/13). These are Riflemen Henry and Philip Bassett of the Queen Victoria's Rifles, both killed on 1st July. Henry was twenty-five, and his brother only twenty; after the war their parents moved to an address in Paris, and one would like to think had more opportunity to visit their sons' graves than most British families.

**Return to the main road** from the cemetery, **turn left** and continue along it until it joins the D.6 Gommecourt-Puisieux road. Ahead of you is now a large wood. Although this wood – Rossignol Wood – never directly featured in the 1st July fighting, it is worthy of some note. Known by the Germans as Copse 125, the German soldier-author Ernst Junger served here in 1918 and published his account of the fighting under the the title *Copse 125*. Rev. Theodore Hardy DSO, MC, a chaplain attached to the 8th Lincolns, won a Victoria Cross near the wood in April 1918; he subsequently died of wounds and is buried at Rouen. Another VC winner, Sergeant Dick Travers DCM,MM, of the 2nd Otago Regiment, New Zealand Forces, known as 'The King of No Man's Land' by his comrades, operated in this area also in April 1918.

Today the wood is private, and visitors are not welcome.

At the D.6 junction, **turn left** in the direction of Gommecourt. From here the road rises upwards and at the top, as the road bends to the right, stop and look to the left. This position gives a good vantage point across the 56th Division battlefield from a German point of view. Felon Trench – attacked by the Rangers on 1st July– was in the field to the right of the road. In the fields on the left was Nameless Farm, a German strongpoint and observation point which looked right across the valley that was No Man's Land – that valley being easily visible from where you are standing. Hebuterne village and church spire are visible in the distance, and to the right Gommecourt Park. Gommecourt village is now dead ahead on the D.6.

**Continue along the road** and just before the village a civilian cemetery appears on the left. **Go up the steps** and **through the gate** to the back; the far left hand corner, near the compost heap, affords good views across the battlefield towards where the LRBs and QVRs attacked on 1st July. There was also a great deal of fighting in this cemetery itself. **Return to the main road** from the cemetery, **go left** and continue into Gommecourt. Follow the D.6 through the village past the church, war memorial and chateau on the left. There are no shops or bars in Gommecourt. On the northern outskirts of the village, on the left, is an uncleared triangle of grassed-over land. In its midst there is a small concrete German observation post, behind what was Foolery Trench; the German front line of 1st July.

You are now approaching the 46th (North Midland) Division sector. The 46th Division was made up of pre-war territorial battalions from Midland county regiments. For 1st July, the leading attack was made by two brigades, 137 and 139; 137 Brigade was recruited from North and South Staffordshire, and 139 comprised four Sherwood Forester battalions. The ground here was flat and there was no cover for the attacking troops; to increase the problems No Man's Land was in places 400-500 yards across. Prior to the attack an advance trench was dug in front of the old British lines, as on the 56th Division front. Due to lack of labour units, this work was carried out by the assaulting battalions up to the eve of the attack, which meant few men had any proper rest or sleep for some time. Rain fell very heavily in the days leading up to 1st July, which turned the British trenches and No Man's Land into a quagmire. Parts of the new jump-off line could not be used, as the sides had fallen in due to the weather.

On the morning of 1st July the Germans bombarded the British front line very heavily until 6.25am, when the final intensity of the British bombardment caused the German gunners to switch their targets to

British battery positions the other side of Foncquevillers. At zero hour the first waves advanced under a heavy smoke barrage, but the Germans were quick to react by shell and machine-gun fire which, as the attack progressed, virtually cut down the third and fourth waves before they could even join in the advance. This meant that by midday, the first waves had only a tenuous foothold in the German front line. A few men got into the support trenches, but were bombed out. A second attack was ordered by the Corps Commander, Lieutenant-General Snow, for 12.15pm. The 46th Division Commander, Major-General M. Stuart-Wortley was against the idea, as so far six battalions had been repulsed and there seemed little chance of pushing on into Gommecourt and meeting up with the 56th Division. Snow persisted and another advance was ordered for the afternoon under a new smoke and artillery barrage. Assembly for this attack proved difficult in the water-logged trenches, but the men were ready come zero hour. Commanders on the ground watched in horror as inadequate smoke screen and bombardment failed to give the protection required and Stuart-Wortley called off the attack. Runners were dispatched to inform the assaulting troops, and all but one got there on time; one unit advanced as ordered and almost every man became a casualty within a few yards of the assembly position.

The attack on Gommecourt had cost the attacking battalions of the 46th Division some 2,455 casualties. Several battalions had in particular suffered badly; the 1/7 Sherwood Foresters lost 409 casualties out of 536 men who went into the attack. In the 1/5 Sherwood Foresters all twenty-four officers became casualties. Five battalion commanders were killed or wounded. It was a total disaster that resulted in a Court of Inquiry to see what had happened. The Division thereafter felt that the events at Gommecourt were a slur on their character, a slur they were not really able to shake off until their brilliant attack on the Canal du Nord in September 1918.

**Continue along the D.6** in the direction of Foncquevillers. Further along on the left is Gommecourt Wood New Cemetery.

## GOMMECOURT WOOD NEW CEMETERY

This cemetery was made after the war by the concentration of a number of battlefield cemeteries made here after Gommecourt was given up by the Germans in February 1917. The majority of these graves, which now form the bulk of the burials in the new cemetery, were men of 46th Division who fell on 1st July 1916. Now there are 682 British graves, fifty-six New Zealand and one Australian in the cemetery. One of the battalion commanders killed at Gommecourt on

1st July is buried here; Lieutenant-Colonel C.E. Boote (II-B-12) died commanding the 1/5 North Staffordshires opposite the aptly named Folly Trench. Boote was a pre-war territorial officer, who had joined the 1/5 as a Major in May 1915. A memorial in the cemetery wall also commemorates the 46th Division and their actions here on 1st July.

Standing on the main steps of the cemetery and looking straight ahead, you are looking right down No Man's Land and over the flat ground where the division advanced. To the right is Gommecourt Wood; about 200 yards in front of it was the German front line. Directly in front of the cemetery was the attack route of the 1/6 South Staffs, who suffered over fifty percent casualties. Sergeant H. Fitzgerald was with his battalion, and gives a not untypical account of the fighting on 1st July:

'I advanced in the front wave and got as far as the German wire which was very thick and not cut. We couldn't get through. The enemy opened machine-gun fire so I got in a shell hole and remained there till dark. The machine-gun was on top of the parapet not in an emplacement. Just at dusk the enemy sent a small party out on each side of us... I gave the order to retire, we helped the wounded out of the hole and made a run for it. The enemy started calling us back saying "Come back you English bastards", "Come back you buggers", a good number shouted in English.'[4]

**Return** to the main Gommecourt-Foncquevillers road, **go left** and continue on into Foncquevillers. Proceed into the centre of the village. It is one of the larger villages in this area, and boasts a Post Office, several shops and bars.

Foncquevillers was known as 'Funky Villas' to British troops during the Great War. Like Hebuterne, it was in fairly good condition even by 1916. The cellars were used for billeting troops and an Advance Dressing Station was established on the western outskirts of the village. The 46th Division established their headquarters in Foncquevillers in June 1916, and as it was about 800 yards from the front line it was quite possible to walk about in the village without being seen by the Germans. A long communication trench named Berlin Street ran from the north-west corner of the village back to Bienvillers-au-Bois, where a Casualty Clearing Station there dealt with many of the wounded that flooded in on 1st July. Placed against the main village war memorial in Foncquevillers is a small portland stone plaque to the North Staffordshire Regiment bearing the simple inscription 'Gommecourt July 1st 1916'.

At the crossroads opposite the war memorial, at the junction of the

**Communication trench in Foncquevillers, one of the many leading to the Britsih Front Line trenches in front of Gommecourt Wood.**

D.6 and D.3, **take the road going north-west** (Rue Bacon) following the green CWGC sign for Foncquevillers Military Cemetery. This is reached further on.

## FONCQUEVILLERS MILITARY CEMETERY

The cemetery was started by French troops, and there were over 300 French graves when British units arrived at Foncquevillers in the summer of 1915. These have now been removed to the French National Cemetery at La Targette, near Arras. The first British burial was Private William Bradley of the 10th (Stockbrokers) Battalion Royal Fusiliers (II-D-2). Bradley was a vicar's son who died aged thirty, on 6th September, 1915. Thereafter Field Ambulances and fighting units used the cemetery until March 1917, and again for a brief period in 1918. After the war, seventy-four graves from the 1916/18 battlefields to the east of Foncquevillers were brought into what is now Plots II and III. Today the cemetery records 625 British burials along with twelve New Zealand, six Australian, two Chinese Labour Corps and fifty-three unknown. Special memorials were erected to two men, known to be buried in the cemetery.

**Foncquevillers Military Cemetery.**
*Julian Sykes*

The vast majority of the graves in the cemetery are from the 46th Division and their attack on Gommecourt. Plot I, Row L, in particular has many such graves from July 1916. The Division was still in the Foncquevillers sector in March 1917, and there are several graves from this period. The only Victoria Cross winner in the 46th Division on 1st July is also buried here. Captain John Leslie Green (II-D-15) was the medical officer of the 1/5 Sherwood Foresters. With so many casualties men like Green had their work cut out on 1st July. The citation for his award reads:

'... for most conspicuous devotion to duty. Although himself wounded, he went to the assistance of an officer who had been wounded and was hung up on the enemy's wire entanglements, and succeeded in dragging him to a shell hole, where he dressed his wounds, notwithstanding that bombs and rifle grenades were thrown at him the whole time. Captain Green then endeavoured to bring the wounded officer into safe cover, and had nearly succeeded in doing so when he himself was killed.'[5]

Green was twenty-six when he died at Gommecourt, and had only been married seven months. His younger brother also served in the 46th Division, and had been killed in the Hohenzollern Redoubt at Loos in October 1915.

After 1st July, the 56th division took over much of the Foncquevillers sector. Having suffered such heavy casualties, the division was reinforced by many different battalions of the London Regiment – often from units not then serving in the division. The graves of these reinforcements, who were killed in the day to day attrition of trench warfare, can be found in Plot I, Rows C and M. Some of these men had only been with their units a few days before they were killed.

Leaving the cemetery, **return to the crossroads** in the village. Go **right here**, following signs on the D.6 for Souastre. Hebuterne is also signposted to the right. Further on in the village, a fork in the road is reached; now follow the **left hand fork** D.28 for Hebuterne. Coming out of Foncquevillers the road rises to a crest. Further on just before reaching a pylon on the right, there is a good viewpoint. From here there are commanding views of the northern part of the Gommecourt Park. This was the sector held by the 1/4 Lincolnshires on 1st July. No attack was made here, where the Lincolns' trenches joined the 1/3 London Regiment opposite the nose of Gommecourt Park at a position known as The Kaiser's Oak.

As the D.28 approaches Hebuterne, the road bends; on the left is a calvary mounted on a grass mound. A rough area of ground, partly wired off and behind the calvary, leads to a British observation post which is usually visible from the road. This is easily reached, although fields and crops should be respected. This area marked the junction of the 46th and 56th Divisions on 1st July. Communication trenches ran to the front line, which was less than a hundred yards away. A small sunken road, also visible to the left, once ran all the way to Foncquevillers and in 1916 led to the front line opposite the Kaiser's Oak in Gommecourt Park. The concrete observation post is of 1918 vintage, and was constructed by the Engineers of the 42nd (East Lancashire) Division. Built on or near the site of a similiar observation point which had existed in 1916, today it equally affords good views directly across to Gommecourt Park, the former site of the Kaiser's Oak and the position known as Z Hedge on trench maps. Looking right from the observation post is the valley where 169 Brigade advanced on Gommecourt on 1st July 1916.

Return to the main road, **turn left** and continue in the direction of

Hebuterne. Once back in the centre of the village **turn right** at the crossroads, following the green CWGC signpost to Hebuterne Military Cemetery, back down Rue de Sailly, and then **right** again up the tree lined lane to Hebuterne Military Cemetery and your vehicle.

READING LIST

Dudley-Ward, C.H.   *The 56th Division* (John Murray 1921)
Smith, A.              *Four Years on the Western Front* (London Stamp
                          Exchange 1987)
Stuart-Dolden, A.   *Cannon Fodder* (Blandford Press 1980)

# THE PALS WALK- SERRE

STARTING POINT:  **Sucrerie Cemetery, Colincamps**
DURATION:  **3 ½ hours**
WALK SUMMARY:  **A walk covering the areas largely associated with the northern Pals battalions of the 31st Division and their actions at Serre on 1st July and 13th November 1916.**

*There is no metalled track leading to Sucrerie Cemetery, and it cannot be reached from Colincamps itself. It is therefore approached from the Mailly-Maillet – Serre road (D.919). Leaving Mailly, just before a cross-roads at the junction of D.174 and D.919, there is a pull-in off the road, with a green CWGC sign for the cemetery. The vehicle may be left here, bearing in mind access to and from the fields by tractors. Leaving your vehicle, continue down the track in the direction of the cemetery, which is visible from the starting point.*

## SUCRERIE MILITARY CEMETERY

Begun by French troops in 1915, British burials in Sucrerie Cemetery started in July 1915 when the 4th Division took over the Serre-Redan Ridge sector. The cemetery was named after a derelict sugar factory located near to the main road. Burials continued until March 1917, and were again numerous in the Spring Offensive of 1918; particularly among New Zealand units which stopped the German advance here. By the Armistice there were 827 British graves, sixty-five New Zealand and two Canadian. The unknowns are 74 in number- a much smaller proportion than in most Somme cemeteries – and

**View towards Sucrerie Cemetery; the former sugar factory was sited just to the right of the track.**

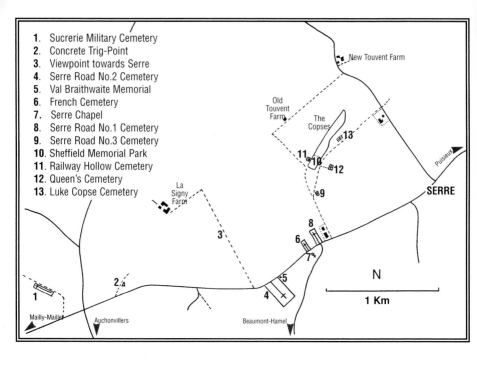

1. Sucrerie Military Cemetery
2. Concrete Trig-Point
3. Viewpoint towards Serre
4. Serre Road No.2 Cemetery
5. Val Braithwaite Memorial
6. French Cemetery
7. Serre Chapel
8. Serre Road No.1 Cemetery
9. Serre Road No.3 Cemetery
10. Sheffield Memorial Park
11. Railway Hollow Cemetery
12. Queen's Cemetery
13. Luke Copse Cemetery

New Touvent Farm

Old Touvent Farm

The Copses

Puisieux

La Signy Farm

SERRE

N

1 Km

Mailly-Maillet    Auchonvillers    Beaumont-Hamel

Special Memorials exist to seven soldiers.

Early graves can be found in Plot III, and there are a large number of 1st July burials. The long tree lined track leading from the cemetery to Colincamps is much as it was in 1916; troops used this as a main route up to the line at Serre, as communication trenches started close to where the cemetery is located. On the eve of the Somme battle several Pals battalions marched up this track and noticed deep trenches had been dug near the earlier burials – fresh graves ready for the forthcoming offensive. The majority of the 1st July graves are from units in the 4th Division who were attacking south of Serre and across Redan Ridge. A number of officers are buried in Plot I, Row H; among them are two battalion commanders. Lieutenant-Colonel The Hon. L.C.W. Palk DSO (I-H-14) died on 1st July aged forty-five while leading his men of the 1st Hampshires into the attack. Buried next to him is Lieutenant-Colonel J.A. Thicknesse (I-H-15); Thicknesse was a year older than Palk and was killed near the Heidenkopf at Serre commanding 1st Somersets; his adjutant Captain C.C. Ford (I-I-67) died with him, but it buried elsewhere in the cemetery. Both Palk and Thicknesse were regular soldiers and they had seen many years of service between them; Palk had been in France since August 1914, and Thicknesse was a veteran of the North West Frontier and South Africa.

Two men who are possibly brothers lie buried here; L/Cpl D.

30

McArthur (I-H-28) and Pte L. McArthur (I-I-69). Both were members of the 2nd Seaforth Highlanders and died on 1st July 1916. A soldier 'shot at dawn' is buried just to the left of the main cemetery entrance; Pte James Crozier (I-A-5) of the 9th Royal Irish Rifles was executed on 27th February 1916. His grave was moved to the cemetery after the war from Mailly-Maillet; for more information on this man see Behind The Lines Walk.

Leaving the cemetery **turn right** onto the track and return to where you are parked. Where the track meets the main road (D.919), **turn left** onto the road in the direction of Serre. Go **straight across** the nearby cross-roads and several hundred yards further up, a concrete trig-point is seen on the left. **Stop**. From here you have a good view across the battlefield. Over to the right distance is Hawthorn Ridge, and the trees of the Hawthorn Crater can be clearly seen. Beyond them to the right are the distant pine trees of the Newfoundland Park. The Thiepval Memorial is also visible on clear days. Ahead the village of Serre can be seen, but before it are the Serre Chapel and areas of the front lines on 1st July. To the left is a large farm complex – La Signy Farm, which in 1916 boasted deep cellars used extensively by British troops in this sector. Continue along the road. As you get nearer to Serre, views towards Redan Ridge on the right get better. The road bends to the right, and then to the left slightly. About a hundred yards before the Serre Road No 2 Cemetery which soon becomes visible, a cart track opens up on the left. Follow this uphill until a high point is reached just before the track drops down into a valley.

There is a superb view from here across to the Pals battlefield area around the copses at Serre. This track was known in 1916 as Sackville Street and communication trenches from the Sucrerie led here. La Signy Farm is behind you to the left. The church spire of Hebuterne is also visible to the north. During the Somme battle a light railway ran the length of the valley, which was dead ground to the German troops at Serre; they could not directly see into it. The railway ran as far as Mark Copse and was used to take up supplies, equipment and on occasion to bring back wounded. On 1st July the dividing line between the 31st Division and the 4th Division ran along the track; some attached units of Royal Warwickshire territorials from the 48th (South Midland) Division formed up here before assaulting the German trenches around the strong point known as the Heidenkopf.

At one time this track turned right at the end and led all the way to the copses at Serre, but part of the track was ploughed up in the late 1980s and there is no longer any access. Therefore return along the track to the main road, and turn left at the end in the direction of Serre

Road No 2 Cemetery. Stay on the main road until the cemetery is reached.

## SERRE ROAD No 2 CEMETERY

This is the largest cemetery on the Somme with 7,139 graves; the division of burials is as follows:

| British | 5,971 | graves, including | 4,287 | unidentified. |
|---|---|---|---|---|
| Canadian | 619 | graves, including | 508 | unidentified. |
| Australian | 401 | graves, including | 72 | unidentified. |
| New Zealand | 73 | graves, including | 29 | unidentified. |
| South African | 34 | graves, including | 24 | unidentified. |
| Newfoundland | 28 | graves, including | 24 | unidentified. |
| German | 13 | graves, including | 6 | unidentified. |

Graves come from all over the 1916 and 1918 Somme battlefields, south of the Somme river and as far away as St Quentin. The original graves are 489 in number, and now form Plots I and II in the centre of the cemetery near the Stone of Remembrance. These burials were made in the Spring of 1917 when V Corps burial parties cleared the Serre-Redan Ridge area; many of them are 1st July casualties or men who died in the second attack on Serre on 13th November 1916. The Essex Regiment is particularly well represented. Isolated graves continued to be brought into the cemetery well into the 1930s, and a few were added after the Second World War.

The large wall at the back of Serre No 2 Cemetery may suggest that War Graves Commission were planning another memorial to the missing here; it is very similar in design to Tyne Cot Memorial in Belgium. The author feels that the planners involved in the construction of the Thiepval Memorial – not completed until 1936 – were worried that they would run out of room on that memorial's panels (as happened with the Menin Gate at Ypres) and considered a possible 'Ancre Heights' memorial at Serre Road No 2 Cemetery; the cut off date between the two memorials being the October 1916 fighting. In the end, all 73,000 names of the Somme missing were included on Thiepval and there are no surviving papers to support the theory that another memorial was planned at Serre.

Among the many interesting burials is the grave of Somme poet Gilbert Waterhouse (I-K-23). Little is known about Waterhouse, except that he was educated at Bancroft School and was commissioned into the Essex Regiment in May 1915. He served in France from 1916 and was killed near the Heidenkopf at Serre on 1st July 1916. A posthumous

**The impressive entrance to Serre Road No.2 Cemetery, the largest British Cemetery on the Somme.**

volume of his poetry entitled *Rail-head, and other poems* was published in late 1916. One of the finest from this collection is 'Bivouacs',

> In Sommecourt Wood, in Sommecourt Wood,
> The nightingales sang all night,
> The stars were tangled in the trees
> And marvellous intricacies
> Of leaf and branch and song and light
> Made magic stir in Sommecourt Wood.
>
> In Sommecourt Wood, in Sommecourt Wood,
> We slithered in a foot of mire,
> The moisture squelching in our boots;
> We stumbled over tangled roots,
> And ruts and stakes and hidden wire,
> Till marvellous intricacies
> Of human speech, in divers keys,
> Made ebb and flow thro' Sommecourt Wood.
>
> In Sommecourt Wood, in Sommecourt Wood,
> We bivouacked and slept the night,
> The nightingales sang the same
> As they had sung before we came.
> 'Mid leaf and branch and song and light

And falling dew and watching star.
And all the million things which are
About us and above us took
No more regard of us than
We take in some small midge's span
Of life, albeit our gunfire shook
The very air in Sommecourt Wood.

In Sommecourt Wood, in Sommecourt Wood,
I rose while all the others slept,
I seized a star-beam and I crept
Along it and more far along
Till I arrived where throbbing song
Of star and bird and wind and rain
Were one – and then I came back again –
But gathered ere I came the dust
Of many stars, and if you must
Know what I wanted with it, here
I keep it as a souvenir
Of that same night in Sommecourt Wood.

In Sommecourt Wood, in Sommecourt Wood,
The cuckoo wakened me at dawn.
The man beside me muttered, "Hell!"
But half a dozen larks as well
Sang in the blue- the curtain drawn
Across where all the stars had been
Was interlaced with tender green,
The birds sang, and I said that if
One didn't wake so cold and stiff
It would be grand in Sommecourt Wood.

\* \* \* \* \* \* \* \* \* \* \* \* \*

And then the man beside me spoke,
But what he said about it broke
The magic spell in Sommecourt Wood.

Waterhouse was one of seven published poets who died on 1st July 1916, four of them here at Serre.

Other interesting graves include a close friend of another poet-Edmund Blunden. Captain Cyril Powys Penruddock (XI-G-1) was

34

killed commanding B Company of the 11th Royal Sussex Regiment at Hamel on 3rd September 1916, aged only twenty. Blunden recalled him in Undertones of War:

'... Penruddock was reckoned rather too young for the command; and, as I see him in the pool of time gone by, he appears as a boy, fair-haired, fine-eyed and independent of experience.' [1]

Elsewhere the grave of a very early Somme casualty can be found; Driver Alfred William Simmons (XII-L-12) was a twenty-seven year old Hackney man serving in the Motor Transport Army Service Corps. He drowned in the river Somme on 24th October 1914. The grave of Pte Albert Edward Bull (XIX-E-16) of the 12th York and Lancs (Sheffield Pals) can also be seen; he died on 1st July and a private memorial to him will be visited later on this walk.

Leaving the cemetery by the main gate, **go right onto the main road**. As the cemetery wall ends on the right hand side, go to a cross on a small mound off the road. It is a private memorial, one of many on the Somme. This one commemorates Valentine Braithwaite, an officer of the 1st Somersets who was killed near this spot on 1st July. Val Braithwaite was a young regular officer who had been in France since 1914, and was mentioned in dispatches for gallantry in the fighting around Ploegsteert ('Plugstreet') Wood in December 1914. The area at the back of his memorial cross is the site of the German defence work known as the Heidenkopf – on British maps it was named the Quadrilateral. The 1st Somersets attacked across this ground on 1st July, and lost heavily from German fire before they even crossed their own trenches; their commanding officer, Lieutenant-Colonel Thicknesse, and adjutant, Captain Ford, were both killed; they are buried in the Sucrerie Cemetery where you were earlier. The fighting in the Heidenkopf became confused, and many officers disappeared never to be seen again; Val Braithwaite was one of them, and his name can be found on the Thiepval Memorial. After the war his well connected parents – his father commanded the 62nd (West Riding) Division in 1917 – erected the memorial on its current site and today it is maintained by the CWGC.

Another 1st Somersets officer who was mortally wounded at Serre on 1st July was Brigadier-General C.B. Prowse DSO. Bertie Prowse was a very popular and highly respected officer who had been Val Braithwaite's company commander in 1914; he later commanded 1st Somersets and by the Somme was Brigadier-General of 11 Brigade, of which 1st Somersets formed a part. Captain G.A. Prideaux witnessed his death:

"... at about 9.45am the General [Prowse] decided to move his headquarters into the German line, thinking that it had been cleared of all Germans. Just as he was getting out of the front-line trench... he was shot in the back by a machine-gun in the Redan Ridge."[2]

Prowse's wound proved serious and he died of his wounds in a Casualty Clearing Station at Vauchelles; he was originally buried in Vauchelles Communal Cemetery, but today his grave can be found in Louvencourt Military Cemetery. Unusually, several places on the Western Front were named after him; Prowse Farm at Ypres, Prowse Point at Ploegsteert (now a military cemetery) and Fort Prowse near Auchonvillers. In that heavy fighting at Serre on 1st July, the 1st Somersets lost twenty-six officers and 438 men killed, wounded and missing.

Leaving the memorial, **return to the main road** and continue in the **direction of Serre**. Further along the Serre French cemetery is reached on the left; opposite the Serre chapel. This cemetery with 817 graves commemorates French soldiers who died in the Serre-Hebuterne sector

**German aerial photograph looking west towards the British trenches at Serre. The distinctive nose-shaped protrusion in the German trenches was known as the Heidenkopf.**
*Klaus Spath*

in 1914/15. Many of the graves are from the fighting around Touvent Farm at Serre in June 1915, and at the back of the cemetery is a fine memorial to men of three French infantry regiments recruited in Lille. Their original shell damaged memorial is just to the right of the modern replacement, which has a beautiful bronze freeze of a French soldier reaching out to Christ. This is a well kept cemetery, and on the second Sunday in June every year a small service of remembrance is held in the Serre chapel opposite. Afterwards a reception is held in Hebuterne- well worth a visit if you are in the area on that day. It usually attracts several hundred people.

Leaving the French cemetery, **turn left** back onto the main road and continue in the direction of Serre. A hundred yards or so on the left, Serre Road No 1 Cemetery is reached.

SERRE ROAD No 1 CEMETERY
Like Serre Road No 2, this cemetery was substantially enlarged after the war. An existing battlefield cemetery made in May 1917 when the ground at Serre was cleared, the original graves are in Plot I, Rows A to G; the majority are 1st July men from the 4th and 31st Divisions. Indeed, many Pals are buried in this cemetery and for a number of years it was the centre for Old Comrades pilgrimages to the area; in particular the Bradford Pals made an annual visit. Now there are 2,106 British burials, along with 149 Australian, 123 Canadian, twenty-seven New Zealand, six South African, one Newfoundland and twenty-two Special Memorials. Most graves, however, are unknowns.

Major J.N. Bromilow (I-B-51) had previously served in the Mediterranean Expeditionary Force before coming to France in May 1916 to take command of 1st King's Own Royal Lancaster Regiment; he died on 1st July. Elsewhere the high price paid in senior Warrant Officers on 1st July is found with two men buried side by side. CSM H.J. Sparks (IV-G-6) and CQMS E. Roberts (IV-G-7) were both regular soldiers of the 2nd Essex Regiment, with many years service between them. Of those burials brought into the cemetery after the war, a frequently visited one commemorates two brothers buried in the same grave. Ptes Charles and Paul Destrube (IV-C-2) were French Canadians serving in a Kitchener's Army battalion- the 22nd Royal Fusiliers. With only a year between their ages, they died together on 17th February 1917.

Leaving the cemetery, return to the main road and **turn left** in the direction of Serre. A large modern farm building is on the left, and where it ends a grouping of familiar green CWGC signposts can be seen. These point up **a track, follow this uphill** until a further cemetery is reached. During ploughing time, there are large numbers of shells and other debris dumped by this track which should be left well alone; some years ago lethal gas canisters were found and just left there for months!

### SERRE ROAD No 3 CEMETERY

This is one of four battlefield cemeteries in the area of the four copses, named from south to north, Matthew, Mark, Luke and John. The British front line ran along their edge in 1916. They were replanted after the war, but Matthew was ploughed up some years ago, and the other three have been planted to become one small wood now.

The northern Pals battalions that fought here on 1st July 1916, although not unique in Kitchener's Army, came to symbolise the sacrifice of the best of a generation in the trenches of the Western Front. Recruited locally, often from small communities, each battalion had its own local character and a wide mix of men from every social class. They had a very high opinion of themselves, but prior to the Somme had served only briefly in Egypt on the Suez Canal and holding the line in quiet  sectors of the Somme battlefield. The majority of these men had little previous military service, but what they lacked in experience they made up with in enthusiasm. Despite this, they fell in their hundreds at Serre on 1st July, and as a consequence many of the northern towns and cities in Yorkshire and Lancashire went into mourning; locals were later to feel that the smaller towns like Accrington were never really to recover from the disaster at Serre. Much has been written about their experiences in recent years, but John Harris' epitaph remains as potent as when he first wrote it in the 1960s,

'... two years in the making, ten minutes in the destroying, that was our history.'

There are good views across the Serre battlefield from this cemetery and the small car-park in front of it. Serre No 3 lies in the former No Man's Land and on 1st July the 15th West Yorks (Leeds Pals) attacked across this ground towards Serre; they lost 528 men in doing so. Behind them were the Bradford Pals of the West Yorkshire Regiment who lost 515 men. Of the eighty-one British graves and four Special Memorials, only thirty-six are to known soldiers. The majority of these are 1st July men, largely from the Leeds Pals.

Leaving the cemetery, **return to the track and turn right**. Almost immediately the track forks; take the **right hand fork** going gradually downhill. Very soon it reaches the edge of Mark Copse, now the Sheffield Memorial Park. You have now moved into the area of the battlefield where the 11th East Lancs (Accrington Pals) fought on 1st

**Looking down the old No Man's Land at Serre towards the Copses – now the Sheffield Memorial Park.**

July. The Park originally only commemorated the 12th York and Lancs (Sheffield Pals), who attacked to the left of the Accrington Pals, but later researchers realised that the small ditch that was once the front line trench was in fact the jumping off position of the Accrington men. Initially amateur military historian John Garwood placed a small plaque on a tree in the Park to the men of the Chorley Company of the 11th East Lancs, but some years later a much larger memorial to all of the Accrington Pals was erected just behind the old trench. The memorial takes the form of a broken down wall, made from Accrington bricks. It is one of several memorials erected by well meaning individuals in the last ten years.

Moving further along the track the main entrance to the Park is reached; a wooden gate that leads you down some steps towards the Sheffield Memorial. The small wooden plaque to the Chorley Pals is on a tree to your left; another similar plaque on the right commemorates the Barnsley Pals. Evidence of old trenches and shell holes are seen among the trees. Over to the right, on the parados of the original front line trench where the Sheffield Pals were on 1st July, is a large concrete cross. This is a memorial to Pte Albert Edward Bull, who was one of 512 casualties in the battalion that day. For many years he was posted missing, believed killed, until his body was found on this spot in 1928. Bull was given a permanent grave in Serre Road No 2 Cemetery, but his family also chose to remember him here. Beyond the main Sheffield Memorial the ground drops away past a huge shell crater. A small cemetery is seen and is reached by a grass path across a field from the park.

## RAILWAY HOLLOW CEMETERY

Another battlefield cemetery, it was made in the spring of 1917 when the area was cleared of isolated graves. It is named after the light railway that ran from near La Signy Farm and which remained in use until the second major action at Serre on 13th November 1916, and again in further fighting in February 1917. Men could walk about quite freely here, un-observed from the German lines. Of the 107 graves in Railway Hollow, most are men who died near here on 1st July. The inscription on Sheffield Pal Alf Goodlad's grave (A-22) quotes from one of his letters home, invoking that 'France is a nation worth fighting for' and has attracted the interest of many visitors. A large number of Accrington and Sheffield men lie here, but other Pals battalions are represented. Two French graves, of soldiers who died in 1915, were retained in the cemetery and are in somewhat poorer condition than their British allies.

Going back through the park and the main gate to the track, go straight over it and up a **grass path across the fields**. This leads to another cemetery and slopes upwards to it, clearly showing the rise up which the Pals attacked on 1st July. It is only slight, but enough when you consider the amount of equipment each man was carrying. Aside from his usual Battle Order, rifle and helmet, many men had picks, shovels, rolls of wire, steel piquets, signalling equipment and the myriad of gear deemed necessary for attacking and holding the German positions. No Man's Land on 1st July was hardly cut up by the bombardment; many accounts mention waist high grass. But that slope looms above you – with the German trenches sited on the crest, looking down on the advancing Pals with a clear field of fire.

## QUEEN'S CEMETERY, PUISIEUX

The third of four battlefield burial grounds, Queen's is very much an Accrington cemetery. There are many Pals buried here whose bodies were not finally laid to rest until May 1917 – nearly a year after their deaths at Serre on 1st July. There are 311 burials, with some from the fighting in November 1916. Among the Accrington Pals is one of their company commanders, Captain Arnold Tough (D-62). The battalion had 585 casualties on 1st July, among them twenty-one officers. The son of the Vicar of Leeds is also buried at Queen's; Lieutenant Stanley Morris Bickersteth (E-19) was killed aged twenty-five, commanding B Company of the Leeds Pals. His father later became Canon of Canterbury and Chaplain to the King. The young Bickersteth had been educated at Rugby and Christ Church College, Oxford; a typical ideal of the sort of officer who died on the First Day of the Somme –

youthful, fit, well educated and from a middle or upper class background.

**Return via the grass path** to the track and **turn right**. The track continues to run along the old No Man's Land and further up on the left another grass path across the fields takes you to the last of the battlefield cemeteries.

## LUKE COPSE CEMETERY

Named after the copse that can be seen from the back of the cemetery, it is close to the front line of 1st July. The layout of the headstones – placed in staggered narrow rows against one wall – perhaps suggests a mass burial when this cemetery was made by battlefield clearance parties in May 1917. Of the seventy-two commemorations, twenty-eight are unknown soldiers. Among the known burials are two brothers from the Sheffield Pals; L/Cpl Frank and Pte William Gunstone. Both joined up together in 1914, and both died on 1st July. They are buried ten headstones from each other. Several men from the Hull Pals battalions of the East Yorkshire Regiment can also be found in this cemetery; they died in the fighting east of Luke Copse on 13th November 1916.

Leave the cemetery by the grass path, and **return to the track**. **Turn left** and continue along it. As the edge of Luke Copse lines up with you on the left, stop and look in a north-eastern direction towards a farm in the near distance. The area bordering the road near this modern farm-New Touvent Farm – is where men of the Hull Pals battalions of the East Yorkshire Regiment fought on 13th November 1916. These men had not taken any significant part in the 1st July fighting, and even by November still fully retained their localised Pals identity. The four battalions raised in Hull between August and November 1914 were

**Men of the Hull Pals marching to the Serre trenches, November 1916.**

recruited almost entirely from local men, and further characterised by their unofficial names; the 10th East Yorks were known as The Hull Commercials, the 11th as The Hull Tradesmen, the 12th as The Hull Sportsmen and the 13th, in typical Yorkshire humour, T'Others! After training at Ripon the four battalions eventually became 92 Infantry Brigade, itself part of the 31st Division, formed entirely of these northern Pals battalions.

On 13th November, as part of a joint attack by the 31st and 3rd Divisions, 92 Brigade took the leading role in the fighting. The 12th and 13th East Yorks were selected as the spearhead battalions, and assembled in the trenches just east of Luke Copse on the night of 12th November. Advance parties of snipers and Lewis gunners were sent out into No Man's Land to cover the attack, which began at 5.45am on the 13th. The 12th East Yorks advanced on the left, in the area around New Touvent Farm, and the 13th on the right, in the pasture south of the road. Moving through a mist, and following a good artillery barrage, the 12th Battalion initially did well. All objectives were taken within twenty minutes, and over 300 men of the 66th Regiment were made prisoners. These were sent back across No Man's Land, but due to the ferocity of the German counter-barrage, only about half made it to the British lines. The 13th had similarly fared well in the initial advance, and bombed their way up support and communication trenches. The Germans put up some resistance but were forced out, often at the point of the bayonet. The support line was reached by both battalions and occupied, but German counter-attacks began later that morning. On the right of the Hull Pals, the 3rd Division had failed badly in their attack, and this left the Yorkshiremen in an exposed and difficult position. On the 12th Battalion front,

"... the trenches had been so blown about that it was impossible to make them really defensive. The Germans counter-attacked in force during the day from the left, but were annihilated by our Lewis guns."[3]

One member of the 12th heavily involved in repelling these counter-attacks was Pte John Cunningham. 'Jack' Cunningham had been born at Scunthorpe in 1897, but his family moved to Hull when he was young and Jack grew up there. He joined the 12th East Yorks in early 1915, when he was only seventeen years old. At Serre on 13th November Jack Cunningham was a company bomber:

'After the enemy's front line had been captured, Pte Cunningham proceeded with a bombing section up a communication trench. Much opposition was encountered, and the rest of the section became casualties. Collecting all the bombs from the casualties, this gallant soldier went on alone. Having expended all his bombs, he returned for a fresh supply and again he proceeded to the communication trench, where he met a party of ten of the enemy. These he killed and cleared the trench up to the enemy line.'[4]

For his gallantry that day, Jack Cunningham was awarded the Victoria Cross, the first Hull man ever to receive the decoration. He was presented with the VC at Buckingham Palace in 1917, but was seriously wounded later in the war. Cunningham had an unhappy life in Hull after the war, and died there after a long illness in 1941.

By the afternoon the situation in the Hull Pals' positions was becoming serious. Lack of men, ammunition and bombs made fending off the counter-attacks difficult and the Germans were massing in even greater numbers. Posts on the 13th Battalion's front were already being overrun; Captain R.M. Wooley, commanding D Company, was in command of one of them:

'We showed ourselves in force, tried to get the Huns who we were fighting to come over but they were strong in number and stout fighters and refused to come. Later, whilst still fighting Huns just in front of us in part of their 3rd line, a man looking out behind warned me. I looked round to find 30 or so of our men (Suffolks) prisoners, coming right on us and before I could do anything Germans coming up behind them and with them in greater numbers were on us, our own captured men prevented my being able to fight without killing them.'[5]

Wooley was wounded in the thigh, and spent the rest of the war in a German Prisoner of War Camp.

By 3pm the Pals were forced to retire to the German front line, and a stand was made so that the wounded could be evacuated back to Luke Copse. A final withdrawal was made after dark, and the front of the 31st Division remained exactly as it had earlier that day. Serre had eluded capture once more. The two battalions from Hull had suffered over 800 casualties between them, with a high proportion of dead among these figures; the 12th East Yorks lost 139 all ranks killed, and the 13th 148. Of these men, over 80% were original 1914 enlistments; Hull had escaped the firestorm of 1st July, but its men were unable to escape a second time. Serre had truly become the graveyard of the Pals battalions.

**Continue along the track**, past another modern farm on the right. The track eventually meets the Serre-Hebuterne road. **Turn left** onto the road. Stay on the road until it bends to the left before the New Touvent Farm. A **track** opens up **on the left**, following the line of some

**Hull Pals: soldiers of the 13th East Yorkshire Regiment (T'Others) in training, 1915. Many of those in this photograph were killed at Serre 13th November 1916.**

pylons. The copses are now also on the left. **Go up this track**, which at first goes uphill. Hebuterne and Gommecourt are visible to the right. Where the track levels out, La Signy Farm can be seen ahead, with the British side of the copses visible on the left. Further along a small group

**The ruins of Touvent Farm in 1915.**
*Julian Sykes*

of trees is on the right, with the remains of an old building. This is the site of the original Touvent Farm, a large complex which was part of the front line in June 1915. There was heavy fighting here between French and German troops, when the farm was captured by the French. The new lines became those taken over by the British in the autumn of 1915, and remained unchanged until 1st July. Nothing remained of Touvent Farm after the war, and it was rebuilt on a new location – which you have just passed to come up this track.

Continue along the track. At a pylon, the **track turns to the left** back towards the copses. Follow it downhill into the valley where the trench railway ran from Mark Copse to La Signy Farm – visible now to the right. At the bottom Railway Hollow Cemetery is seen on your left, and the track now veers off uphill to the right. Matthew Copse was once in the field to the left of this track. Continue until it reaches the junction of tracks near the car park of Serre Road No 3 Cemetery. Go back down the track from Serre Road No 3, rejoining the main D.919 road from Serre to Mailly. **Turn right** where track meets road, and stay on the road now, past all the places visited earlier in the walk. Walking at an average pace, it takes about forty minutes to get back to the Sucrerie Cemetery and where your vehicle is parked. Past Serre Road No 2 Cemetery, there are good views to the left across the Beaumont-Auchonvillers battlefield.

## READING LIST

Cooksey, J.    *Barnsley Pals*  (Pen & Sword 1986,1988,1996)
Garwood, J.    *Chorley Pals*  (Richardson Publishing 1989)
Gibson, R.    *Sheffield City Battalion*  (Wharncliffe Publishing 1988)
& Oldfield, P.
Harris, J.    *Covenant With Death*  (Hutchinson 1961)
Horsfall, J.    *Battleground Europe: Serre* (Pen & Sword 1996)
& Cave, N. (Ed)
Milner, L.    *Leeds Pals*  (Pen & Sword 1991)
Turner, W.    *Accrington Pals*  (Pen & Sword 1987,1992)

# BEAUMONT-HAMEL

STARTING POINT: **Church, Auchonvillers**
DURATION: **2 ¹/₂ hours**
WALK SUMMARY: **A fairly short walk, ideal for those who have
limited time or are inexperienced walkers. The walk makes an in-
depth study of the Auchonvillers-Beaumont-Hamel sector, with
particular reference to the fighting on 1st July 1916 and the actions
of the 29th Division.**

*Park your vehicle to the side of the church, in the centre of
Auchonvillers. The church is located in a road which becomes a cul-de-
sac, and there is no problem parking here.*

The first part of this walk follows a route taken by Great War poet
Edmund Blunden in September 1916, and is described in Chapter Ten,
'A Home from Home', of *Undertones of War*. Blunden was then field
works officer to his battalion – the 11th Royal Sussex Regiment (1st
South Downs). Auchonvillers or 'Ocean Villas', as the British troops
called it then, was almost in ruins by the time Blunden came to the
village. Among the rubble of the church was a huge bell, used locally
as a gas alarm. The cellars of nearby houses were being used as stores
and dugouts, and a large one near to the church was an officer's billet.
An Advanced Dressing Station was located on the western outskirts of
the village, just off the Mailly-Maillet road. Trench mortars had
positions in and around the village, which by the time of the Battle of
the Somme had been turned into a veritable fortress.

Leaving the church, **go south to the cross-roads** in the centre of the
village. At the cross-roads go **straight across**, following signs for the
D.73 to Hamel, down Rue Delattre. Pass a water tower on the right, and
farm buildings to the left. On the outskirts of the village is a large
tarmaced area in front of a farm, again on the left. **Move onto this
tarmac**, which opens up to reveal the start of a cart track. This is the
entrance to the Old Beaumont Road. Blunden's 1916 walk took him
down Rue Delattre, where you have just been, to the start of this road.
On the way he noticed piles of trench mortar ammunition, and coming
into the sunken part of the Old Beaumont Road picked a blackberry
from some brambles.

**Go down the Old Beaumont Road**. It is sunken at first and then
after a hundred yards or so the banks on the right end and there is a

**The ruins of Auchonvillers Church, 1915.**

**Auchonvillers: the ruined school teacher's house being used as an observation post by a French officer.**

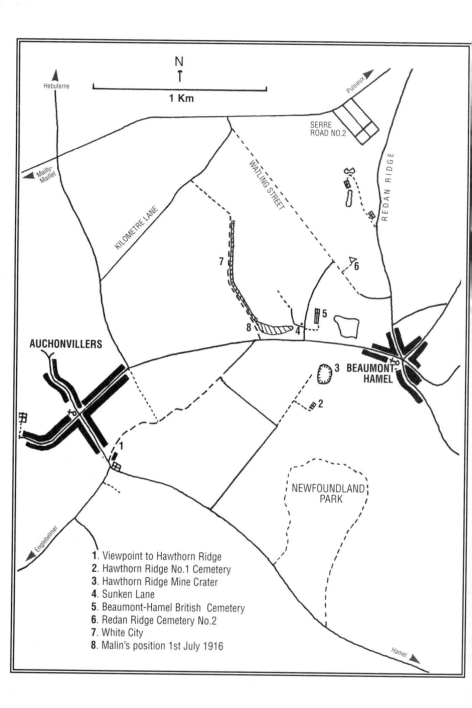

**N**

1 Km

Hebuterne

Mailly-
Maillet

Puisieux

SERRE
ROAD No.2

REDAN RIDGE

WATLING STREET

KILOMETRE LANE

7

6

5

8       4

AUCHONVILLERS

3 BEAUMONT-
HAMEL

2

1

Englebelmer

NEWFOUNDLAND
PARK

Hamel

**1**. Viewpoint to Hawthorn Ridge
**2**. Hawthorn Ridge No.1 Cemetery
**3**. Hawthorn Ridge Mine Crater
**4**. Sunken Lane
**5**. Beaumont-Hamel British  Cemetery
**6**. Redan Ridge Cemetery No.2
**7**. White City
**8**. Malin's position 1st July 1916

clear view across to the right. **Stop here**. A system of communication trenches, known on British trench maps as Avenues and numbered one to five, ran in this sector taking battalions up to the front line. Second Avenue began just to the right of where you are now, following the line of the track. A trench railway ran in a specially constructed gully out in the fields on the right, going from behind Auchonvillers right up to the support lines on Hawthorn Ridge. The Ridge itself is also visible from here; the German lines were beyond the trees of the Hawthorn mine crater, on the left, and behind Hawthorn Ridge Cemetery No.1 – the two distinctive trees in the cemetery are seen on the skyline of the ridge. Edmund Blunden entered Second Avenue at this point; at night men did chance a walk along the cart track, but as can be clearly seen in daylight anyone here would have been visible from the German lines and so the usual route up to the trenches was by communication trench. Although Second Avenue has long since been filled in, the Old Beaumont Road has changed little since 1916. Considering it was a main route up to the line, from which many did not return, this part of the walk has a particular poignancy.

**Continue along the Old Beaumont Road**. Further along it bends to the right, and becomes partially sunken again. Past the turn, it bends again to the left and straightens out for a while. On a third bend to the right, there is a scrub area on a small bank on the right. This was the location of a large dugout that served as battalion headquarters for units in the line on Hawthorn Ridge. Blunden's walk ended here, where he reported to his commanding officer, Lieutenant-Colonel G.H. Harrison DSO. Where this area of scrub ends, a cart track slopes up to the fields. Second Avenue trench went up here and continued on to the front line on Hawthorn Ridge. To the left, in a large open field, a trench named 88 Trench ran directly north to the main Auchonvillers-Beaumont-Hamel road, and beyond it to a wood known as The Bowery; which was never replanted after the war and there is no sign of it today. Blunden slept in a dugout off 88 Trench where the 11th Royal Sussex had their Regimental Aid Post (RAP). This RAP had been originally constructed for the 1st July offensive, when RAMC men from the 29th Division handled many of the wounded from Hawthorn Ridge here on that day. Afterwards the RAP was handed over in turn to each unit coming into the sector.

**Continue** to follow the track of the Old Beaumont Road. There are now high banks on the right, which in 1916 were riddled with dugouts. You are also now out of view from Hawthorn Ridge, which is over to the right. Stay on the track until it becomes metalled, and the new road winds off to the right. **Take this road to the right**, going uphill onto

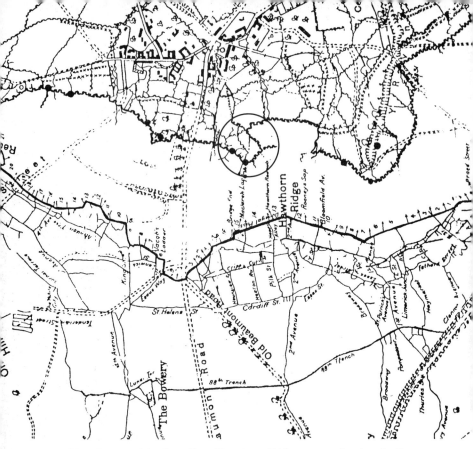

**Trench map of Auchonvillers-Hawthorn Ridge sector, showing the lines as they were before 1st July 1916.**

Hawthorn Ridge. This is a modern road, made after the Second World War providing an access route to Hawthorn Ridge Cemetery. As you move away from the Old Beaumont Road, in 1916 communication trenches ran at angles across this road to the front line. One of them was named Heaton Road, after Second Lieutenant Eric Heaton, a young officer of the 16th Middlesex Regiment (Public Schools Battalion); possibly he and his platoon dug or improved the trench in the months leading up to 1st July. The dominance of Hawthorn Ridge becomes apparent as you climb it by this road. The British lines were in the fields to the left and right. The German lines lay over the crest of the ridge just ahead; the trees of the Hawthorn mine crater are on the skyline to the left, and Hawthorn Ridge No 1 Cemetery to the right of the crater. Further right trees on the outskirts of The Newfoundland Park are visible.

**Follow the road** to the top, where it joins a track to the left and

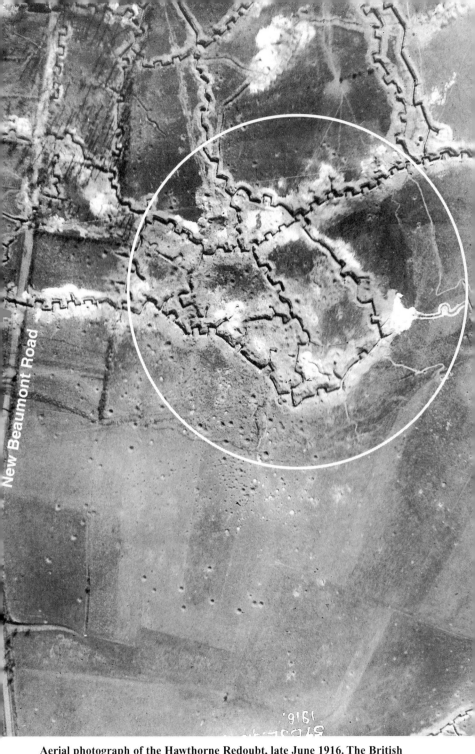

Aerial photograph of the Hawthorne Redoubt, late June 1916. The British front line can be seen at the bottom right.

Y Ravine

Hawthorn Redoubt

New Beaumont Road

British Front Line

British Front Line

Old Beaumont Road

Sunken Lane

British Front Line

**German aerial view of the Beaumont Hamel Battlefield looking south, taken late June 1916. Y Ravine is visible towards the top of the photograph; the old Beaumont Road snakes off to the right.**
*Klaus Spath*

**German trenches in the Hawthorn Redoubt; their depth is particularly noticeable in this photograph.**
*Klaus Spath*

continues as a metalled road to the right. **Stop here** and look back. You are now looking across the area over which men of the 29th Division attacked on 1st July 1916. This Division was a regular army one, and many of its battalions had been in India or Ireland on the outbreak of war. They formed in England and in 1915 fought at Gallipoli where the Division became known as 'The Immortal 29th'. The division came to France in April 1916 and took over the line in and around Auchonvillers. The Hawthorn Ridge sector became the responsibility of the 86th Brigade; made up of 2nd Royal Fusiliers, 1st Lancashire Fusiliers, 16th Middlesex Regiment (Public Schools) and 1st Royal Dublin Fusiliers. All but the Middlesex had been with the 29th since the outbreak of war; the Public Schools Battalion had previously been on lines of communication duties, and had seen little front line service. Commanded by a regular officer, Lieutenant-Colonel Hamilton Hall, they were a keen and much liked battalion in the division.

On 1st July, 86 Brigade was allocated the ground from the trenches east of the area known as White City across to Hawthorn Ridge. Taking the metalled road which you have just walked up as twelve o'clock, to the right at about two o'clock, a track winds up to a position out of view from Hawthorn Ridge; this was the wartime location of White City; an area of dugouts, RAPs and dumps which were screened from German observation by large chalk spoil banks (gleaming white- thus the name). The British front line prior to 1st July was to the right, in what are now ploughed fields. At certain times of the year chalk marks of old trenches are visible. Following the line of these fields, a large white celtic cross is seen – this marks the entrance to the famous Sunken Lane, occupied by 1st Lancashire Fusiliers on 1st July. Further mention of this will be made later in the walk. As the positions on Hawthorn Ridge were so strong it was decided that a huge land mine containing 40,000lbs of Ammonal explosive would be used to assist in the attack. The 252nd Tunnelling Company Royal Engineers was brought in to carry out the task which involved digging galleries and shafts across No Man's Land and under the German trenches. The explosive charge would then be laid, and blown at some point in the opening phase of the advance. A tunnel out towards Hawthorn Ridge was started early in 1916, which began in the British lines near the old

Beaumont Road. Pte Horace Ham of the 16th Middlesex was attached to the tunnellers on several occasions,

> '... when we came out of the line, we'd go back to our billets. You're supposed to go out for a rest, but they came round about eight at night and said "You, you, you – come on, fatigues up the line"... The entrance to the tunnel was in a reserve trench, just under the parapet, and went at an angle. We used to go down this bloomin' long shaft, which had been dug by the miners. There was electric light down there and they had a fellow at the top, turning a wheel, working a pump, sending the air down, and we brought up sacks of earth and emptied them over the top at night.'[1]

The mine was eventually exploded at 7.20am on 1st July, some ten minutes before zero hour. Its detonation signalled the first phase of the attack. A small advance party of men from the 2nd Royal Fusiliers under Captain Russel, along with machine-gun and trench mortar units, rushed the near lip of the still smoking crater. However, the Germans had emerged from their dugouts in double quick time, and so were already in position. Machine-gun fire raked Russel and his men, cutting down members of the carrying party, struggling across No Man's Land with a heavy load of trench mortar ammunition. The survivors reached the British lip of the crater, fired off what ammunition they had and held on till 7.30am and beyond, hoping they would be re-supplied in the main advance. In most places the German wire was uncut and even undamaged. The attacking battalions were mown down by the waiting machine-guns; the main body of the 2nd Royal Fusiliers melted under

**The Hawthorn mine is blown at 7.20 am, 1st July 1916.**

murderous fire from the Hawthorn Redoubt, suffering terrible
casualties. Russel and his men at the crater could do nothing but watch
in horror at the spectacle before them. Captain G.V. Goodcliffe of 2nd
Royal Fusiliers only lived to relate his story because he was in reserve
and watching the fighting:

'The attack was a hopeless failure. As far as I know no-one
reached the Bosche front line except a few odd men where the
mine was blown. Col. Johnson O.C. the Bn was buried and
wounded by one of our own shells – fired by the 6 inch S.African
Battery. He was dug out in our front line and still attempted to
command. During the Battle it was my duty to command the 10%

Soldiers of the 119 RIR's machine-gun section who occupied a dugout in the Hawthorn Redoubt on the morning of 1st July 1916. Those marked with a cross were among twenty-eight men killed in the mine explosion.
*Klaus Spath*

A view inside the Hawthorn mine crater taken 2nd July 1916 by an officer of 119 RIR who had successfully defended it the day before.
*Klaus Spath*

[those left behind in reserve] and occupy the Bosche front line when captured. In order to obtain information as to the situation I examined our wounded when they returned. One man, who saw what I was doing, came up to give me his news. His lower jaw was shattered but he insisted on telling me his story in spite of it all. Owing to his wound he was very difficult to understand but went on mumbling until he made me understand his news which was – "we are doing no good on the right". When I repeated the message he nodded, smiled (as far as a man in his state could smile) and went off to the dressing station. Of all the officers that went over the top only two did not become casualties – Dearden and Baldwin, of whom the former had his steel helmet dented by a shell. For 48 hours after the battle wounded came dribbling in – several of them mad. The Bosche came out of their trenches under cover of a Red Cross flag and collected some of our wounded. They 'played the game' except I saw them remove Lewis guns on stretchers.'[2]

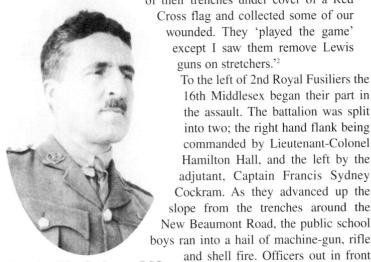

**Captain F.S. Cockram DSO, 16th Middlesex, who was '...hit three times... finally he fell riddled with bullets'.**

*Cockram Family*

To the left of 2nd Royal Fusiliers the 16th Middlesex began their part in the assault. The battalion was split into two; the right hand flank being commanded by Lieutenant-Colonel Hamilton Hall, and the left by the adjutant, Captain Francis Sydney Cockram. As they advanced up the slope from the trenches around the New Beaumont Road, the public school boys ran into a hail of machine-gun, rifle and shell fire. Officers out in front leading their men fell everywhere. Platoons and companies were decimated. The survivors were pinned down, but still their courage and determination led them on:

'... the 16th Middlesex moved forward to the left very steadily and reached the crater though not without considerable loss. Here their adjutant Captain Cockram made a gallant attempt to initiate a further advance, he was hit three times, on each occasion regaining his feet and leading the advance; finally he fell riddled with bullets.'[3]

But Captain Cockram was not dead. His battered and torn body was discovered around the lip of the mine crater by German stretcher bearers later in the day and he was taken prisoner, spending the remainder of the war in several hospitals and prisoner of war camps, ending up in a hospital camp in Switzerland. Lieutenant-Colonel Hamilton Hall strongly recommended him for the Victoria Cross, but he later received a Distinguished Service Order in the New Year's Honours list for 1917. After the war he returned to his native London, married and had two daughters, and despite the severity of his wounds lived to the age of eighty-two.

Another of the Middlesex officers hit in the attack was Second-Lieutenant Eric Rupert Heaton. This was the young officer who had worked on Heaton Street trench with his men, near the Old Beaumont Road. He had written to his parents on 28th June, while the battalion was in bivouacs at Auchonvillers:

'I am writing this on the eve of my first action. Tomorrow we go to the attack in the greatest battle the British Army has ever fought. I cannot quite express my feelings on this night and I cannot tell you if it is God's will that I shall come through but if I fall in battle then I have

**Second Lieutenant Eric Rupert Heaton, 16th Middlesex Regiment, KIA 1st July 1916.**

no regrets save for my loved ones I leave behind. It is a great cause and I came out willingly to serve my King and Country. My greatest concern is that I may have the courage and determination necessary to lead my platoon well. No-one had such parents as you have been to me giving me such splendid opportunities and always thinking of my welfare at great self sacrifice to yourselves. My life has been full of faults, but I have tried at all times to live as a man and thus follow the example of my father. This life abroad has taught me many things chiefly the fine character of the British race to put up with hardships with wonderful cheerfulness. How I have learnt to love my men; my great aim has been to win their respect which I trust I have accomplished and hope that when the time comes I shall not fail them.If I fall do not let things be black for you, be cheerful and you will be living then always to my memory.'[4]

In the advance on Hawthorn Ridge Eric Heaton was wounded in the

**The Heaton family visit Eric Heaton's original grave on Hawthorn Ridge 1919. The small plaque which they placed against his cross is just visible; it is still there today.**

leg, fell into the long grass only a few yards from the mine crater, and was never seen alive again. For months he was reported missing, and there was still some faint hope among his family that he had been taken prisoner like Captain Cockram and perhaps lost his memory. However, when the Somme battle was over, Heaton's body was found by a burial detail and the agonising wait for his parents had ended. The whole Heaton family visited the grave in 1919 and left a small plaque, which is still there today, in Hawthorn Ridge No.1 Cemetery. Heaton was one of twenty-two officers and 517 men of the 16th Middlesex to become casualties that day. The 2nd Royal Fusiliers had suffered even worse casualties: twenty-three officers and 538 men.

From this vantage point **follow a cart-track northwards** towards the Hawthorn mine crater. A hundred or so yards further on, past a small concrete pylon, there is a green CWGC sign pointing across the fields to Hawthorn Ridge Cemetery No.1.

## HAWTHORN RIDGE No.1 CEMETERY

This cemetery was one of a number created by V Corps burial details in the Spring of 1917, after the Germans had withdrawn to the Hindenburg Line. The Ancre battlefield was systematically searched

**Hawthorn Ridge Cemetery No.1.**

for isolated graves and bodies of British soldiers, and several small 'comrades' style cemeteries were made. The graves in Hawthorn Ridge No.1 came largely from the Hawthorn Ridge area and Beaumont-Hamel – many were found around the mine crater only about a hundred yards from the cemetery. There are 152 British and one Newfoundland burials here; among them are seventy-one unknowns. The majority of the graves date from 1st July 1916, and are largely men of the 29th Division which attacked across Hawthorn Ridge that morning. Of the 153 graves, some forty-two are of men from the 16th Middlesex Regiment, who assaulted the mine crater. Several of their officers are buried here, among them the young Second-Lieutenant Eric Heaton (A-89) who died aged only twenty. There are two other officers: Lieutenant Henry James Heath MC (A-84) and Captain George Henry Heslop (B-40). The names of other 16th Middlesex men in the two rows of graves indicate varied backgrounds: Bonnici (A-67) from Malta, De Silva (A-51) who came from Ceylon to enlist, Durell (A-7) a vicar's son, and Hosking (A-45) a student at the Royal College of Music.

Other interesting 29th Division graves include A/Bdr H.J. Brockett of B Battery RHA (B-34), who must have been on Forward Observation duties when he died on 1st July 1916. Cpl H.C.S. Rees (A-68) was a member of 2nd Monmouths, the Divisional Pioneers, and was part of a group from that unit which rushed the crater at zero hour. The graves of 4th Division men, such as Pte J.W. Burton 1st East Lancs (A-59) may well have been found in Beaumont village, as the Redan Ridge group of cemeteries largely cover the men from that division. The graves from when this position was captured by the 51st (Highland) Division on 13th November 1916 number six; most of whom are from the 1/5th Seaforths. 1918 graves are very few- and are largely of men killed holding the line when this sector settled down to its former 1916-trench lines after the March Offensive. A puzzling grave of an unknown East Yorkshire Regiment man lies in B-55; his date of death is recorded as 5th September 1918 – when the fighting was miles away, beyond Bapaume – and may be the date his body was found rather than when he actually died. Quiet and rarely visited, the views from this cemetery are spectacular.

Leave the cemetery by the grass lane, and **rejoin the track**. A detour to the right can be made to have a closer inspection of the Hawthorn mine crater, but there is little to see and access to the crater from this side is restricted by barbed wire fences. Otherwise, **turn left** onto the track and return to the junction of track and metalled road. **Turn right**, back down the hill following the road you came up earlier. At the bottom, where the road becomes part of the Old Beaumont Road, **turn right** and follow until it meets the New Beaumont Road (D.163). **Turn right onto the main road** heading in the direction of Beaumont-

**View from the German front line trenches opposite the Sunken Lane looking directly down the New Beaumont Road towards Auchonvillers.**
*Klaus Spath*

**Men of the 1st Lancashire Fusiliers in the Sunken Lane on the morning of 1st July 1916.**

Hamel. A few hundred yards further up towards the village, **a track** appears **on the left**; take this turning which brings you to the start of the Sunken Lane.

The Sunken Lane was actually in No Man's Land prior to 1st July; the British front line was to the left of the lane towards White City. Sappers of 252nd Tunnelling Company RE dug a tunnel, which ran from the British trenches into the Sunken Lane. In the early hours of 1st July advance parties of the 1st Lancashire Fusiliers, Trench Mortar Battery men and Machine-gunners made their way into the lane; the idea was that attacking from here would considerably cut down the distance across No Man's Land. The Official Cinema-tographer, Geoffrey Malins, did some filming in the Sunken Lane just after dawn on 1st July, which later appeared in the *Battle of the Somme* film. Those assembled here would have witnessed the explosion of the Hawthorn mine as they waited to go over, and at zero hour leapt out of the Sunken Lane and attacked across the ground to the right of the lane towards a small wood on the outskirts of Beaumont-Hamel. In this short distance murderous machine-gun fire from trenches in front of the wood and enfilade fire from Beaumont-Hamel village and Hawthorn ridge cut the 1st Lancashire Fusiliers down like corn. It was a proud battalion, led by their charismatic commanding officer Lieutenant-Colonel Meredith Magniac; men who had fought their way up the beaches and cliffs of Gallipoli, and had achieved immortal fame for winning 'Six VCs before breakfast' in the original landings, melted away into machine-gun oblivion. Magniac somehow survived, and was awarded the Distinguished Service Order for his bravery and leadership that day, but was tragically killed at Arras the following year. Casualties amongst Magniac's men on 1st July were high: eighteen officers and 465 other ranks were killed, wounded or missing.

After 1st July the Sunken Lane was annexed by the British and a new trench dug along the right hand lip, called Hunter Trench. This became the new front line, and it was from here that the 1/8th Argyll and Sutherland Highlanders successfully advanced on Beaumont-Hamel on 13th November 1916. The white celtic cross at the entrance to the lane is their massive battalion memorial. **Before going up the Sunken Lane turn right** along a grass lane which leads to Beaumont-Hamel British Cemetery.

## BEAUMONT-HAMEL BRITISH CEMETERY

Like the one on Hawthorn Ridge this cemetery was started in November 1916 when burial details of the 51st (Highland) Division cleared the battlefield around Beaumont-Hamel. The majority of the graves are men who fell on 1st July. Burials continued into 1917; a few were added after the war. The cemetery now commemorates 111 British soldiers, one Canadian and one Newfoundlander. Among them are sixty-three unknown soldiers, and two Special Memorials. Of the 1st July graves in this cemetery many are men of the 1st Lancashire Fusiliers who fell crossing this ground. One of their officers is buried here; Second-Lieutenant A.F.D. Anderson (A-6), an Australian, was aged twenty-two when he was killed at Beaumont-Hamel on 1st July. Elsewhere a 16th Middlesex officer can be found; Lieutenant Frederick Tanqueray (B-62) was serving in B Company, and died aged twenty-four. Lieutenant S. Mc Donald Campbell (B-52) was a Lancashire Fusilier officer who commanded the 86th Brigade Trench Mortar Battery on 1st July and was one of the few men who reached the lip of the mine crater, where his body was found after the battle.

**Return** via the grass lane, and **turn right up the Sunken Lane**. In winter months a deep impression can be seen on the left bank; this was the tunnel exit that ran from the British trenches near White City. In the right bank are entrances to old British dugouts, one of which collapsed in 1994. They are dangerous and should not be entered. **Continue** up the lane until it is no longer sunken and becomes a cart track. This track eventually meets another; turn right here and follow this track towards Beaumont-Hamel. A military cemetery is seen on the left; **take the grass lane** from the track you are on which leads to the cemetery.

## REDAN RIDGE CEMETERY No.2

Another battlefield cemetery from November 1916, the graves here are again largely men who fell on 1st July. You have now moved out of the 29th Division's area of operations into the 4th Division area on Redan Ridge. This was another regular army division, which had been in France since August 1914; it suffered heavy casualties in trying unsuccessfully to cross Redan Ridge and take the German lines north of Beaumont-Hamel. The cemetery is, in fact, a mass burial. The registers records 279 British soldiers, 124 of them unknowns; some of the headstones commemorate more than one man. The largest concentration of graves are from 1st Hampshires; fifty-seven of their graves can be found here. There are are also twenty men of the 1st Lancashire Fusiliers. This gives the cemetery very much a regular army feel. Along these lines, among the known graves are three Drummers;

**White City 1st July 1916: Packed with troops waiting to take part in the offensive. These are men of the 1st East Lancs; the officer on the left touching the brim of his cap is Second Lieutenant N.F. Currall who was later killed in action on 18th October 1916.**

*Frank & Lou Stockdale*

Dmr A.J. Lakin (C-18) and Dmr W. Morgan (C-14) both of the 1st Lancashire Fusiliers, and Dmr H. Toomer (B-100) of the 1st Hampshires. All three died on 1st July. There is an intriguing inscription on the grave of Captain E.G. Matthey (C-44) another 1st Lancashire Fusiliers man; it reads "Tikkah" and one can only assume this was perhaps a family nick-name ?

Leaving the cemetery, return to the track by the grass lane across the field. **Where lane meets track turn right**. On British maps this track was known as Watling Street. It will lead you away from the battle area, and occasionally it pays to stop and look back at the views. Eventually Watling Street meets a metalled track which it joins just south of the

main D.919 Mailly-Maillet-Serre road. This metalled road was in 1916 Kilometre Lane; **turn left onto it** and follow gradually downhill. Again there are good views across the battlefield; Auchonvillers is ahead in the distance. Follow Kilometre Lane for a few hundred yards until a track appears on the left hand side. **Take this track**, which will now lead you to the White City area. The track runs straight until it reaches the conclusion of another; **turn right** onto this track and head due south. Banks will begin on the left, and get higher the further you walk along. Further up is a quarry. **Stop here**.

Up until 1995 there was a small area of scrub in a field opposite the quarry, directly bordering the track. Where you are now was the area known as White City. There were large sandbagged dugouts, cut into the chalk banks. Dumps of ammunition and equipment were also located here and the area of scrub marked the location of an Advanced

Dressing Station known as Tenderloin. A large underground ADS, this was the main evacuation route for men wounded in the Sunken Lane and on Redan Ridge. They would have been taken back along Fourth or Fifth Avenue communication trenches down to a Main Dressing Station in Mailly-Maillet, and then further back to a Casualty Clearing Station at Forceville or Louvencourt (there are military cemeteries in both of these villages where evacuated men died of wounds). The cinematographer Geoffrey Malins, and his colleague Lieutenant Brookes, an official photographer, were busy in this area both before and on 1st July 1916, taking much film footage and many photographs. A number of these have become classic images of the Great War. The dugouts and dumps at White City were used throughout the Battle of the Somme, and many units had their headquarters here.

**Continue along the track**; it bends to the left further on and eventually the bank on the left turns left on a corner towards the Sunken Lane. Near this corner Malins and Brookes were installed in their dugouts, awaiting the explosion of the Hawthorn mine on 1st July. Malins later recorded:

> '... the ground where I stood gave a mighty convulsion. It rocked and swayed. I gripped hold of my tripod to steady myself. Then, for all the world like a gigantic sponge, the earth rose in the air to the height of hundreds of feet. Higher and higher it rose, and with a horrible, grinding roar the earth fell back upon itself, leaving in its place a mountain of smoke.'[5]

Going to the edge of this corner, it is possible to line up almost exactly the images Malins and Brookes took that morning.

**Continue along the track** until it meets the main Beaumont-Hamel -Auchonvillers road (D.163). Turn right onto the road, and follow it back into Auchonvillers. Further along, before it meets the Hebuterne road (D.174), turn and look back – there are good views towards the Hawthorn Ridge battlefield and many of the areas visited on the walk. Continue along the D.163 into Auchonvillers. The cross-roads in the village is soon reached; **turn right** for the church and your vehicle.

### READING LIST

Ashurst, G.    *My Bit. A Lancashire Fusilier at War* (Crowood Press1987)
Blunden, E.    *Undertones of War* (Cobden-Sanderson 1928)
Cave, N.        *Battleground Europe: Beaumont Hamel* (Pen and Sword 1994)
Malins, G.    *How I Filmed The War* (Herbert Jenkins 1920)

# ANCRE VALLEY

STARTING POINT:  **Car Park, Newfoundland Park**
DURATION:  **3 hours [depending on time spent in Newfoundland Park]**
WALK SUMMARY: **This walk gives time to explore the Newfoundland Park in some detail. It then takes the walker on some pleasant walks around the Ancre Valley, many of which command spectacular views over the 1916 battlefields.**

*Newfoundland Park is well signposted from both Auchonvillers and Hamel. A car park is outside the main entrance. Go into the park by the main gate. A memorial is ahead of you to the left. This granite obelisk mounted on a bed of flowers and bush is the memorial to the 29th Division. It bears the red triangle, which was the divisional sign.*

A regular army division, the 29th was formed in England by a concentration of regular infantry battalions that returned from India and other outposts of the Empire. In April 1915 it took part in the landings at Gallipoli and in much of the later fighting on the Peninsula, where it became known as the 'Immortal 29th'. The division came to France in April 1916, taking over trenches in the Beaumont-Hamel sector. It remained here until the operations on 1st July, when the divisional front spanned from the Sunken Lane at Beaumont-Hamel to the trenches south of where the Newfoundland Park is today. Casualties in the 29th Division on 1st July 1916 amounted to 223 officers and 5,107 other ranks.

**Continue along the main path** which leads up to the Caribou memorial. A flight of steps is seen on the left; take these and follow the route up to the viewing platform just below the Caribou. This memorial commemorates men of the Newfoundland Regiment who died here on 1st July. In 1914, Newfoundland was a self-governing colony (it is now part of Canada) and in terms of population the smallest to raise its own regiment. The originals came to England, and joined the 29th Division at Gallipoli towards the end of 1915. They came to the Western Front in the spring of 1916, and fought here at Beaumont-Hamel on 1st July. They went on to fight at Guedecourt, Monchy-le-Preux, Ypres, Cambrai and Courtrai- similar Caribou monuments are located on these battle sites, although the Newfoundland Park remains the largest single memorial to the 'Gallant Newfoundlanders'. Bronze panels below the Caribou commemorate men of the regiment, and the Newfoundland

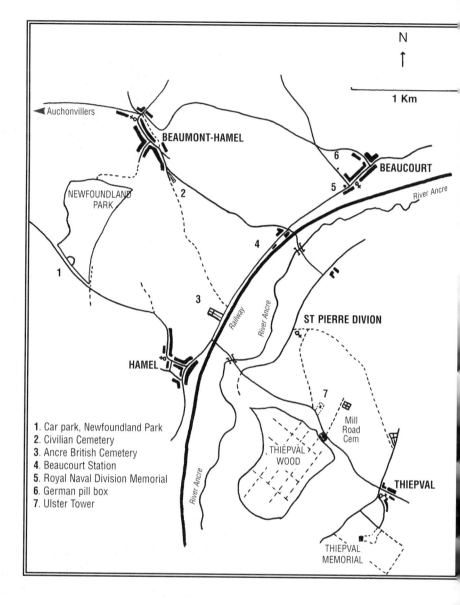

1. Car park, Newfoundland Park
2. Civilian Cemetery
3. Ancre British Cemetery
4. Beaucourt Station
5. Royal Naval Division Memorial
6. German pill box
7. Ulster Tower

Mercantile Marine, who have no known grave.

On the morning of 1st July the Newfoundland Regiment was in reserve, in trenches close to the Hamel-Auchonvillers road. After the first waves had left the front line, and were cut down by lethal German fire from Beaumont-Hamel, the Newfoundlanders were called up with the 1st Essex to follow the attack. The communication trenches leading to the front line were already clogged with the wounded from the first

The 29th Division memorial at the entrance to Newfoundland Park in the 1920s.

The original warden's house in Newfoundland Park under construction in the early 1920s. It was replaced by a more modern building after the Second World War.

**The Caribou Memorial.**

wave, which made movement difficult. The Essex kept to the trenches, but the commander of the Newfoundland Regiment ordered his men up into the open, so they could reach the British front line more easily. However, the Newfoundlanders could now be seen from the German lines near the Y Ravine and men began to fall even before the jumping off positions were reached. The battalion's War Diary recalls a chilling tale:

'... the heaviest casualties occurred on passing through gaps in our own wire where the men were mown down in heaps... In spite of the losses the survivors steadily advanced until close to the enemy's wire by which time very few remained.'[1]

Photographic evidence from German sources shows that some men – whether from the first wave or the Newfoundland Regiment – got into the German lines near the Y Ravine, but they were small in number and were surrounded, killed or taken prisoner. The casualties among the Newfoundlanders had been heavy – twenty-six officers and 658 men had been killed, wounded or missing. The Newfoundland Regiment had all but ceased to exist. Among the dead were four members of the Ayre family; L/Cpl Edward Ayre (Y Ravine Cemetery; A-33), Captain Eric Ayre (Ancre British Cemetery; II-E-12), 2/Lt Gerald Ayre (Commemorated on the Caribou Memorial) and 2/Lt

**Captain Eric S. Ayre**
**Newfoundland Regt**
**KIA 1st July 1916**

70

W.D. Ayre (Knightsbridge Cemetery; B-10). A fifth member of the family, Captain Bernard Ayre, was also killed on 1st July with the 8th Norfolks; he is buried at Carnoy Military Cemetery (see Montauban Walk).

**2/Lt William Ayre**
**Newfoundland Regt**
**KIA 1st July 1916**

There are good views across the park from the viewing platform, and the warden's house can be seen over to the right; this is the home of Steve Austin Jnr who has followed in his father's footsteps in becoming custodian of the Newfoundland Park. Steve is an enthusiastic and knowledgeable character, and despite being a very busy man is always pleased to answer visitor's enquiries. It is hoped that a visitor's centre will open in the park in 1997. There is no specific route to follow in the park and you are at leisure to explore the place; you will be leaving the park from near the 51st (Highland) Division memorial in the distance, so it is wise to end up near there. Otherwise the following cemeteries and memorials can be visited:

## Y RAVINE CEMETERY

One of three military cemeteries in the confines of the park, the burials were made in November 1916 when the pioneer battalion of the 51st Division cleared this part of the Beaumont-Hamel battlefield. They found the bodies of many soldiers who had fallen on 1st July, and had lain out in No Man's Land ever since; many of the headstones in the cemetery bear two names, reflecting the nature of this mass burial. There are 328 British graves, thirty-eight Newfoundland and sixty-one Special Memorials. One of the famous Newfoundland Ayre family is buried here; L/Cpl Edward Alphonsus Ayre (A-33) was killed on 1st July, aged only nineteen. Many other 29th Division men lie in this cemetery, among them CSM J.S. Fairbrass of the 2nd South Wales Borderers (C-66). Fairbrass came from a large military family from Westcliffe-on-Sea; six brothers served and three of them died in the war. A number of Royal Naval Division graves from the Beaucourt fighting can also be found in Y Ravine Cemetery.

## HUNTERS CEMETERY

This unique circular cemetery was a mass grave made in an old shell hole after the capture of Beaumont-Hamel on 13th November 1916. All of the forty-six burials are men from units in the 51st Division which fought here on that day.

## 51ST (HIGHLAND) DIVISION MEMORIAL

Close to Hunters Cemetery, this fine memorial commemorates the capture of Beaumont-Hamel and the ground beyond by the 51st Division in November 1916. The superb bronze surmounting the monument is said to be of a well-known RSM in the division, a holder of the DCM and MM. Whatever, the gaelic inscription sums up much of the fighting on the Somme, or indeed in any war; 'Friends are good on the day of battle'. Nearby, a wooden cross also recalls the division's engagement at High Wood in August 1916.

## HAWTHORN RIDGE No 2 CEMETERY

Another cemetery created when the Ancre battlefields were cleared in the Spring of 1917, it is close to Hawthorn Ridge- which can be seen across the fields to the rear of the cemetery. The majority of the 214 graves are of men who died on 1st July; all but twenty-three are British, the remainder Newfoundland.

## Y RAVINE

This deep natural feature is believed locally to be an old quarry. It runs, snake-like, from the rear of what in 1916 was the German front line, all the way back to the village of Beaumont-Hamel. The ground from the German trenches slopes down to the Ravine, and from the

**German aerial view of the area, part of which now forms Newfoundland Park. Ringed area is Y Ravine.** *Klaus Spath*

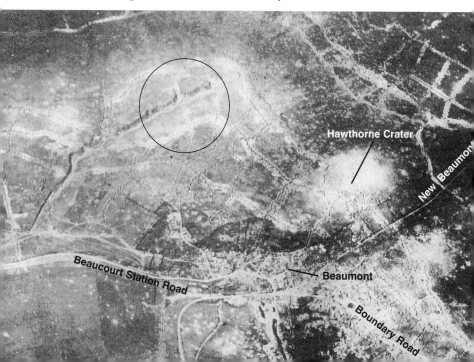

**British dead in Y Ravine. This photograph was taken by an officer of 119 RIR 1st July 1916.** *Klaus Spath*

British lines in 1916 German soldiers could not be seen from either here or in the Ravine itself. The sides of the Y Ravine were honeycombed with dugouts, many of them reinforced with concrete. Tunnels ran from the Ravine up to the German trenches, and one was found in 1994. It is hoped that at some stage the tunnel system might be opened to visitors.

Evidence suggests that some British soldiers fought their way into the Y Ravine on 1st July, but were either killed or taken prisoner. The position was not finally taken until the 51st Division swept across this ground on 13th November during their successful advance on Beaumont-Hamel. Today tunnel entrances, trenches and dugouts are still in evidence; although most have fallen in. It is quite possible to get down into the Y Ravine, but the sides are steep and visitors do so at their own risk. One can no longer walk the length of the ravine into Beaumont-Hamel, as the Newfoundland Park boundary fence cuts across it further up and the remainder of Y Ravine is in private hands.

Standing at the rear of the 51st Division memorial, and looking across the Y Ravine, the park boundary fence is visible. A gap in the fence can clearly be seen at the back of the ravine, with a track going across the fields. This is the rear exit of the park; make for this. At the gate, **continue along the track**, which further up turns to the left into

73

Beaumont-Hamel. Here it goes downhill and becomes sunken. During the war this was a common route for German soldiers and ration parties both up to and from the trenches on Hawthorn Ridge. As you go further into the village, steep banks at the rear of farm buildings and houses will be seen over to the left. The Germans constructed wooden chalets into these in 1915/16, and there were tunnels from here running up to the ridge. One wooden construction incorporated the village church bell, and was used as a gas alarm. The 119th Reserve Infantry Regiment of the German army occupied Beaumont-Hamel from 1915, and it was common practice for them to keep the bulk of their forces in deep dugouts and positions in the village, and move them up to the trenches via these tunnels in case of attacks. This proved to be the case on 1st July. Many locals remember these tunnels, and legend has it that they are still there.

**As you come into the village**, the road passes through farm buildings and at the bottom joins the main Beaumont-Hamel-Beaucourt road (D.163E). **Turn right** onto this road and continue to the edge of the village. The road will become forked; the left fork is the continuation of the D.163E to Beaucourt, the right is a minor road leading to the local civilian cemetery. Take the **right hand fork** and continue on past the cemetery, passing it on the left. The minor road soon becomes a cart track, and rises uphill. This was an area of German

**The ruins of Beaumont-Hamel village mid 1916.**

74

support trenches in 1916, and the Y Ravine comes out near to the cemetery you have just passed. Much of the ground round about has not been ploughed since the war, and there are many indentations where once there were dugouts and gun positions.

There is a good view to the left down the Beaucourt Road, known as Station Road in 1916. The chalk cliffs of Beaumont-Hamel quarry are clearly visible, and again they were full of dugouts during the war. RAMC units of the 51st Division established an Advanced Dressing Station along these far banks in the winter of 1916. Author Henry Williamson was also here about that time, serving as a transport officer in the 208th Company Machine Gun Corps. He gives a vivid description of the area and conditions in one volume of his fictionalised autobiography, *Love and The Loveless*[2]. **Continue uphill** on the track. Crossing over the crest and eventually going back downhill again, there are spectacular views across the Ancre valley. The valley winds towards Beaucourt to the left, whilst beyond the village of Thiepval and the Thiepval Memorial can be seen. **Follow the track** down to the main Hamel-Beaucourt road (D.50), and **turn right**. Less than a hundred yards on the right is the elevated and impressive entrance to the Ancre British Cemetery.

## ANCRE BRITISH CEMETERY

This is another concentration cemetery from the Ancre fighting of 1916. The original cemetery (now Plots I and V) was started by V Corps burial parties in the Spring of 1917. It was known as the Ancre River No 1 British Cemetery and contained 517 graves, mostly from the 36th (Ulster) and 63rd (Royal Naval) Divisions. After the war the cemetery was expanded by the concentration of 1,965 graves from the Ancre valley battlefields and today there are 2,446 British burials, thirty-two Newfoundland, two New Zealand and one South African. About half of the graves are unknown soldiers, and in addition there are forty-nine Special Memorials.

One of the Ayre family from the Newfoundland Regiment is buried here; Captain Eric S. Ayre (II-E-12) died on 1st July, aged twenty-seven. Elsewhere in the cemetery there are many graves of officers from the Royal Naval Division, a good many of whom had previously served at Gallipoli. Perhaps the most frequently visited is Lieutenant Hon. Vere Sidney

**Grave of Hon. Vere Harmsworth, KIA 13th November 1916**

**Ancre River No.1 Cemetery: after the war it was expanded to become Ancre British Cemetery. The graves above now form Plot I. In 1916 the German front line ran along the high ground to the rear of these graves.**

Harmsworth (V-E-19) of the Hawke Battalion. Harmsworth was a great friend of Winston Churchill and the poet A.P. Herbert who wrote the immortal poem 'Beaucourt Revisited', and later a book about the Beaucourt fighting, *The Secret Battle*. Vere Harmsworth, the second son of Lord Rothermere and a nephew of Lord Northcliffe, was only twenty-one when he was killed on 13th November 1916. Prior to the Ancre fighting he had been offered a Staff job, but had refused stating the '... greatest honour an officer can receive is to lead his men over the parapet'[3]. In the attack Vere was wounded twice before reaching the German third line where a shell fell close and killed him outright. Two brothers are also buried in the cemetery; Ptes James (I-B-11) and Martin (VII-C-22) Ford were both killed on 1st July with the 1st Royal Inniskilling Fusiliers, aged twenty-one and twenty-two respectively.

Going to the back of the cemetery, a small gully is visible going north in the direction of the Newfoundland Park. This was No Man's Land on 1st July, with the German trenches on the high ground to the right. Elements of the 36th (Ulster) Division attacked across it that day-with little success and heavy casualties. Another attack took place here on 3rd September 1916 when Edmund Blunden's battalion – the 11th Royal Sussex Regiment (1st South Downs) – tried to advance across the gully in difficult conditions. Sergeant William Booth MM was there:

'We were told to go over at 5.10am... and so with as cheerful a word as possible to all near me, came the barrage, when the heavens seem to be alight. We climbed out and moved forward, our loads restricting our movements. I had told our fellows not to fix bayonets until they got in the gully for fear of slipping on to one if they slid down the bank.We all seemed to have survived the first move and it was now just starting to get light across the gully... [there was] no sign of the ladders we had so carefully stowed there. Jerry had found them and carried them off. We were now faced with the task of climbing this bank without ladders.

After climbing and slipping down several times... most of the platoon were up. As we moved there was a sudden silence. The barrage had lifted on, and now we tried to run, but before I could get to the trench, or what was left of it, I caught my foot in the wire.'[4]

Booth was wounded in this costly and unsuccessful attack; a few yards away his brother was struck and killed by a shell. His body was never found, but many of Booth's comrades who died trying to get up the gully are buried in Ancre British Cemetery.

Leaving the cemetery by the main gate, **turn left** onto the D.50 and stay on the main road. Follow towards Beaucourt. This was the attack route of the 63rd (Royal Naval) Division (RND) on 13th November 1916. The RND had originated as an idea of Winston Churchill, when in 1914 there had been a surplus of Royal Naval Volunteer Reservists. He proposed to form an infantry division out of them and Royal Marine units; the division first saw action at Ostend in October 1914, and later suffered heavy casualties at Gallipoli. Several of the original Naval battalions were disbanded due to heavy losses, and when the RND came to France in early 1916 the missing units were replaced by a number of army battalions.

The attack on Beaucourt by the RND was their first major operation on the Western Front. Fighting continued until 15th November, but Beaucourt station and village were successfully captured along with some of the high ground beyond. Casualties amounted to 4,000 all ranks- with nearly 1,600 of the RND killed in action. There were many acts of gallantry during the fighting, and one resulted in the award of the Victoria Cross. Lieutenant-Colonel Bernard C. Freyberg was a New Zealander who had been in London on the outbreak of war in August 1914. Friendly with Winston Churchill, Freyberg managed to secure a commission in the Hood Battalion of the RND. He served at Gallipoli, and was a pall-bearer at Rupert Brooke's funeral in April 1915. For his bravery at Gallipoli Freyberg had been awarded the Distinguished Service Order, and by the Somme was commanding Hood Battalion His Victoria Cross citation reads,

'By his splendid personal gallantry he carried the initial attack straight through the enemy's front system of trenches. Owing to mist and heavy fire of all descriptions, Lieut-Colonel Freyberg's command was much disorganised after the capture of the first objective. He personally rallied and re-formed his men, including men from other units who had become intermixed.

He inspired all with his own contempt of danger. At the appointed time he led his men to the successful assault of the second objective, many prisoners being captured.

During the advance he was twice wounded. He again rallied and re-formed all who were with him, and although unsupported in a very advanced position, he held his ground for the remainder of the day, and throughout the night, under heavy artillery and machine-gun fire. When reinforced on the following morning, he organised the attack on a strongly-fortified village [Beaucourt] and showed a fine example of dash in personally leading the assault, capturing the village and five hundred prisoners. In this operation he was again wounded. Later in the afternoon he was again wounded severely, but refused to leave the line till he had issued final instructions.The personality, valour and utter contempt of danger on the part of this single officer enabled the lodgement in the most advanced objective of the Corps to be permanently held.'[5]

Freyberg went on to be again wounded in other actions of the war, and to add a further two bars to his DSO. He rose to high command in the Second World War, was commander in chief of British forces on Crete in 1941 and in later life was governor-general of New Zealand.

**Continue along the D.50** towards Beaucourt. The now disused railway station of Beaucourt-Hamel will be passed on the right, and further along a **cross-roads** will be reached. **Go straight across** on the D.50 for Beaucourt-sur-l'Ancre. This part of the road has high banks on the left. As these fall away on the outskirts of Beaucourt village, the road will curve slightly and on the left up another bank is the memorial to the Royal Naval Division. This memorial was erected in the 1920s in memory of the Division's first major action on the Western Front here at Beaucourt. It is a large white portland stone obelisk, with bronze plaques. One bears the cap badges of all the units in the RND. For many years it was the only RND memorial in France, until one commemorating the fighting at Arras was erected in the village of Gavrelle in the late 1980s; it is of a very different design to this one at Beaucourt.

Just on the other side of the RND Memorial is a minor road going left off the main D.50 with a no entry sign with the legend 'Sauf Riverains' beneath. There is no trouble for access on foot, and **follow this road uphill**. Modern farm buildings and stables will be passed on the right. Beyond them, again on the right, is a grassed over area with barbed-wire fencing around it. **Follow this fence** as the road continues to rise, until the fence ends just before a field. Close to this corner and behind the barbed-wire is a rare example of a German concrete pillbox; few were ever constructed on the Somme front. Although with the facilities to take a machine-gun, it is more likely that it was used by the Germans for observation purposes. Just turning to the left and seeing the commanding views across the Ancre valley will confirm this to any visitor. The whole of the battlefield around Thiepval can be clearly seen, along with the Ancre marshes, the Newfoundland Park and Hawthorn Ridge.

The farm which you passed on the way up to this pillbox was the 1916 site of Beaucourt chateau. The desire by the British to knock this position out is shown by the number of large calibre shells to be seen lying around nearby. In 1994 the current owners of the farm unearthed an enormous fifteen-inch British shell – the first example of this size of shell to be found in the area for many years. The owners also told the author that the tunnels from Beaucourt chateau were still intact, although very dangerous, and that a few years ago the body of a German sniper was found near the pillbox complete with his steel body-armour and sniper's rifle! All this ground is in private hands, and should be respected.

Leaving the pillbox **return to the D.50** back down the minor road. **Turn right** onto the main road at the RND Memorial, and follow the D.50 back to the cross-roads at Beaucourt-Hamel station. Once here **turn left**, and follow the road over the railway line. The road continues and soon crosses the river Ancre. Carry on further, past the marshes until the road reaches a T-junction. **Turn right** here onto the D.163E for

St Pierre-Divion. You are now in the Ancre valley and behind the German lines prior to 1st July. There were dugouts in the banks nearby, and a large German communication trench ran along the top of the high bank on the left, running back towards Grandcourt.

**Stay on the D.163E** and follow it to the outskirts of St Pierre-Divion. A track will soon appear on the left, and among the trees – also to the left – is the village church. Turn onto this track and follow it alongside the church, now on your right. Just past the church another track snakes off to the right; follow it. This was known as Thiepval Road on British maps, and ran behind and then up to the main German lines opposite Thiepval Wood. Men of the 36th (Ulster) Division attacked towards this ground on 1st July, but the area was only finally taken by units of the 39th Division – with the assistance of tanks – on 13th November 1916. St Pierre-Divion itself was captured by the 1/6th Cheshires and 4/5th Black Watch, aided by 16th Sherwood Foresters. A large number of prisoners were taken. **Stay on this track** as it goes uphill. Occasionally looking back, there are superb views across the Ancre valley. The village of Hamel can be seen to the left, the Newfoundland Park on the horizon and much of the ground over which you have previously walked is visible to the right. The view generally gets better the further up the track you go. Ahead of you up the track

**Ulster Tower Memorial in the 1920s.**

the Ulster Tower memorial will become visible. A few hundred yards before it on the left, just off the track in the field, are the remains of a small German concrete observation post. This is on the site of the former German front line of 1st July, and on the tip of a salient of trenches known to the British as The Pope's Nose. It had good views across to the British lines in Thiepval Wood. Today it is often a dumping ground for unexploded shells and grenades, which should be left well alone. Continue up the track until the Ulster Tower is reached.

The Ulster Tower is a copy of Helen's Tower at Clandeboyne near Belfast, where some units of the 36th Division trained in 1914. It was erected after the war as a memorial to the thousands of men from the division who died on the Western Front, and in particular those who died at Thiepval on 1st July 1916. It is located on the site of the front line trench attacked by the 9th Royal Irish Rifles, and for many years entry to the memorial was only possible by obtaining a key from the keeper in Hamel. The Tower is now owned by the Somme Association; sadly access to the top of the memorial is prohibited, but a room containing plaques and wreaths may still be seen at the bottom. To the rear of the Ulster Tower new buildings house a visitor's centre, tea room and good toilets. This is open every day, except Sundays and Mondays, and is staffed by local French people who speak little or no English. A slide show about the Ulster Division and a small display of artefacts are also worth a look. In and around the grounds are a number of new memorials; one commemorates the Victoria Cross winners of the division, while a more recent one outside the main gate is in memory of the men and women of the Orange Order who died in all twentieth century conflicts.

Leaving the Ulster Tower by the gate, **turn right** onto the main road (D.73) and follow it downhill. It is partially sunken at first, and again there are good views across the Ancre valley. At the bottom of the hill, the ground levels out around the marshes, and the bubbling Ancre itself is crossed on the first bridge. Further on the road crosses the main railway line, and just over it reaches the D.50 Hamel-Beaucourt road. The Ancre British Cemetery, where you were earlier, is visible over to the right. **Turn left** here into Hamel village. As you come into Hamel, the road bends to the right and a junction is soon reached. **Turn right** here onto the D.73 following signposts to Auchonvillers and the Newfoundland Park. The road winds up through Hamel village, and gets steeper as it passes the church on the left. On a hot day climbing this hill can be hard going; as it reaches the top, the local cemetery is on the left. Opposite on the right, just off the road and near a barbed wire fence is a stand-pipe. Although it is not safe to drink, the author

# THIEPVAL

STARTING POINT: **Authuille Military Cemetery, Authuille**
DURATION: **5 hours**
WALK SUMMARY: **A long but rewarding walk covering the whole 1st July sector around Thiepval; the areas fought over, by amongst others, the 8th, 32nd, 36th (Ulster) and 49th (West Riding) Divisions are all seen on this walk.**

*Authuille Military Cemetery is reached from the main D.151 running south through Authuille village; it is clearly sign-posted with a green CWGC sign. Follow a local road downhill into Rue d'En Bas, another CWGC sign is seen on the large barn ahead. Drive down this minor road and park on the grass verge in front of the path leading to the cemetery.*

## AUTHUILLE MILITARY CEMETERY

This is a good starting place for the walk, as the cemetery reflects well the fighting around Thiepval with a mixture of units and dates. There are lovely views here across the Ancre valley towards Aveluy Wood. The graves are on a downward slope and arranged very attractively in this beautiful setting. Charles Douie, an officer in the 1st Dorsets, stood on this spot in the Spring of 1916:

**Charles Douie**

'I stood there looking over the broad marshes of the Ancre and the great mass of Aveluy Wood beyond. There was a lull in the firing, and everything was still. The sun was setting... the river and marshes were a sea of gold, and the trees of the wood were tinged with fore... shadows were lengthening in the woods and on the marshes. A cool evening breeze blew gently through the graves of our dead.'[1]

The cemetery was begun in August 1915 and used by Field Ambulances and fighting units, bringing their dead back from the Thiepval trenches, until December 1916. At the end of the war the cemetery contained then, as now, 451 British graves, fourteen Indian and three South African. Among them there is a strong representation from units in the 32nd, 36th (Ulster) and 49th (West Riding) Divisions which were the key formations involved in the fighting around Thiepval in July 1916. Earlier graves are from when the 51st (Highland) Division held the Thiepval trenches in the latter months of 1915.

The cemetery register records that Lieutenant Stafford Dudley

83

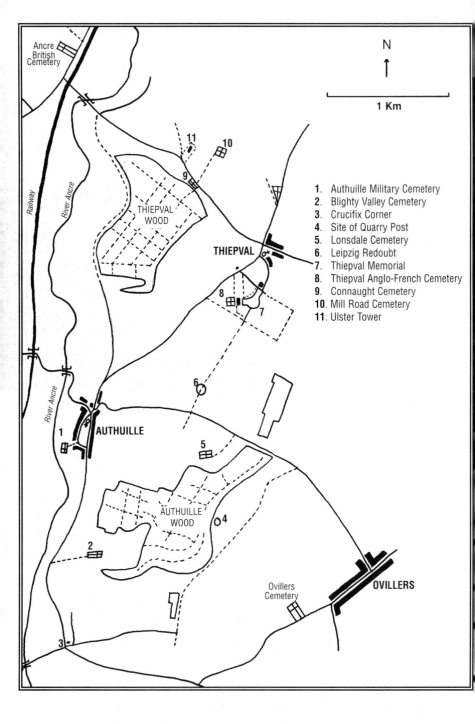

N

1 Km

1. Authuille Military Cemetery
2. Blighty Valley Cemetery
3. Crucifix Corner
4. Site of Quarry Post
5. Lonsdale Cemetery
6. Leipzig Redoubt
7. Thiepval Memorial
8. Thiepval Anglo-French Cemetery
9. Connaught Cemetery
10. Mill Road Cemetery
11. Ulster Tower

Ancre British Cemetery

Railway

River Ancre

THIEPVAL WOOD

THIEPVAL

River Ancre

AUTHUILLE

AUTHUILLE WOOD

Ovillers Cemetery

OVILLERS

**Authuille Military Cemetery.**

Somerville (G-12) of 5th KOYLI was killed in action on 5th July 1916. It further records that his father, Lieutenant-Colonel Stafford James Somerville died in August 1917 whilst commanding the 9th Royal Irish Rifles; he is buried in Brandhoek New Military Cemetery No 3 in Belgium. A row of men from Charles Douie's 1st Dorsets can be found from A-13; in fact this is a mass burial, with the officer buried in A-13 and all the other ranks recorded as being buried in A-14. Douie visited the graves in 1916:

> 'here above the Ancre lie many of the most gallant of my regiment, men who were my friends, men whose memory I shall revere to the end of time. Some of them were soldiers by profession; others had turned aside from their chosen avocations in obedience to a call which might not be denied... they have passed into silence. We hear their voices no more. Yet it must be that somewhere the music of those voices linger...'[2]

If anywhere those voices may be heard in this quiet graveyard, rarely visited by modern pilgrims to the Somme battlefields.

Leaving the cemetery, **follow Rue d'En Bas back onto the main road** where you turned off. Where it meets the main road, **turn right** onto the D.151 in the direction of Aveluy. Further up as you turn the corner, Aveluy church is seen in the distance, and even further on the flash of gold from the Madonna of the Basilica in Albert is sometimes visible. **Stay on the road** until a green CWGC sign for Blighty Valley Cemetery appears on the left. **Follow the grass path** across the fields up the valley to the cemetery.

## BLIGHTY VALLEY CEMETERY

Blighty Valley is a gradual valley running south-west from and through Authuille Wood to the river Ancre between the villages of

**Blighty Valley Cemetery.**

Aveluy to the south, and Authuille to the north. Although shielded from direct view by the Germans, it was only a short distance from the front line and regularly shelled. After the Somme battle began Royal Engineer units laid a light railway along its length, and it became an important route to the front line. As the battle progressed, many units bivouaced here on their way to the trenches. The cemetery was begun in the Summer of 1916 and located some distance from the main Authuille-Aveluy road, towards the mouth of the valley. Used throughout the 1916 battle, the original graves – some 223 in number – made up what is now Plot I. After the war the cemetery was enlarged by the addition of burials from the surrounding battlefields, the majority of whom were men who fell on 1st July 1916. The only major graveyard concentrated into Blighty Valley

was Quarry Post Cemetery at Authuille Wood. On the south edge of the wood, it was used in 1916/17, chiefly by units of the 12th (Eastern) Division. There were once fifty burials there. A Special Memorial also exists close to the entrance of the cemetery to five men buried in Becourt German Cemetery in the Spring of 1918 whose graves could not be later found. Burials in Blighty Valley today number 993 British, two Australian and two Canadian. There are 532 unknowns, with twenty-four Special Memorials.

The earliest grave is that of Pte Ronald Bradbury of 11th Sherwood Foresters (II-B-5) who was killed on 28th June 1916. The majority of the graves here reflect the fighting around Thiepval, Ovillers and La Boisselle. Most are of men who fell in the first week of July 1916 and many are from units of the 70th Brigade, temporarily attached to the 8th Division for the assault on Ovillers. At one time a wooden cross memorial to this brigade existed in the cemetery. Thus a large number of men from 8th KOYLI, who were killed in Mash Valley, are in Plot V, and a similar grouping of men from 8th and 9th York and Lancs can be found in Plot V, Row C and surrounding; among them is the commanding officer of 8th York and Lancs, Lieutenant-Colonel B.L. Maddison (I-B-5) and his adjutant, Lieutenant S. Dawson (V-C-36). There are three other battalion commanders: Lieutenant-Colonel W.S. Brown of the Wiltshires (III-B-7) was killed on 6th July aged forty-six; Lieutenant-Colonel C.G. Forsyth DSO of 6th Yorkshires (I-F-13) fell on 14th September at the young age of twenty-nine and Lieutenant-Colonel W.B. Gibbs (I-D-36) of the 3rd Worcesters died of wounds on 3rd September. The ironically named RSM W.H. Fear of 1/8th West Yorks (I-A-6) was one of that rare breed of Warrant Officers to have been awarded the Military Cross. He was killed near Thiepval on 14th July. Other interesting gallantry winners include two sergeants of 8th KOYLI: Sgt T. Priestley's DCM and MM were gazetted posthumously (III-J-1) and Sgt J.T. Waldron (V-G-17) had been awarded his DCM for gallantry in 1915. A few graves exist from the 1918 Spring Offensive, and those from the August 1918 fighting are largely units in the 38th (Welsh) Division.

**Grave of Lt-Col B.L. Maddison, killed commanding 8th York and Lancs, 1st July**

**Return to the main road** via the grass path, and **turn left** continuing in the direction of Aveluy. The road weaves from here, and the fields drop away into the Ancre valley on the right. Much of this ground was flooded in the latter stages of the battle. Just after the final bend on the left is a large unsightly scrapyard; this is in a disused quarry that was here during the Great War. Thankfully the trees obscure most of the view. Beyond this is a road junction, where D.151 meets the D.20; right is the tree-lined road to Aveluy across the Ancre marshes, and left Ovillers is sign-posted. On the corner of the junction to the left is a wooden bench, often obscured by road materials. Behind it is some woodland and just inside it a large modern crucifix. This is the site of the most famous Crucifix Corner; a main route up to the front lines around Thiepval, Authuille Wood and Ovillers. George Coppard, then a soldier in the 37th Company Machine Gun Corps, came here on the afternoon of 1st July, while the battle was raging around Thiepval:

' There was a terrific crowd of troops and vehicles at Crucifix Corner. The road forked there and in the angle, commanding the approach, stood a huge crucifix. The sorrowful face of Christ gazed down at the turmoil below. I remember looking at His face- a glance only – there was no time for more. Many men, who had passed by on their way to the front not many hours before, were now dead; and many more were to follow them.'[3]

Among the trees are signs of shell holes and trenches, and concrete and brick blocks; possibly an old smashed dugout.

**Return to the road junction, turning left** in the direction of Ovillers on the D.20. Immediately on the left a metalled track will be seen running upwards along the woodland in which the crucifix stands. Ignore the main road and **follow this track**. As it climbs, ignore a fork to the left and continue straight on as the track climbs the hill. Taking

**View towards Aveluy from Crucifix Corner, taken by a German officer in March 1918 when the British front line was on the other side of the flooded Ancre.**

time to look back as you go will afford good views of the Ancre valley; from left to right – Albert, the Golden Virgin of the Basilica, Aveluy and beyond, the Bouzincourt Ridge. **Continuing along the track**, Authuille Wood becomes visible on the left and beyond it the towering frame of the Thiepval memorial above the tree line. At the top the track reaches a T-junction of tracks; **turn left** onto the cart track, no longer metalled. This track now runs through the edge of a small copse.

The 8th Division held this sector and attacked from it on 1st July. The area before the copse was known as Donnet Post and was a reserve position from which the 2nd Rifle Brigade moved up to the fighting north of Ovillers on the morning of 1st July. The front lines were over the rise to Ovillers on the right. **Continue**. Further along, as the track comes out of the copse, it is partially sunken where it meets the southern tip of Authuille Wood. Trees overhang it, making it dark even on a bright Summer's day. Signs of shell holes and trenches can be seen among the trees, but the wood is on private ground and should not be entered. Again, this was a reserve position with dugouts in the banks and the front line some distance to the right of the track; the 11th Sherwood Foresters formed up in the wood here as a reserve battalion on 1st July 1916. As the track itself emerges from the copse, a valley opens up ahead to the left. The view on a summer's day is spectacular – and the pillars of the Thiepval memorial are again seen above the trees. As you move further along the track an area of rough ground maybe seen down in the valley. This is the site of Quarry Post; an Advanced Dressing Station, battalion headquarters and reserve position in the Authuille Wood sector. The 9th York and Lancaster Regiment were at Quarry Post before going into the attack at Nab Valley. A cemetery was also established here, but the graves removed to Blighty Valley Cemetery after the war. Quarry Post is on private land, and cannot easily be reached. **Further along the track**, past Quarry Post, the front line was above the bank and across the high ground on the right; the 8th KOYLI went into the attack here on 1st July suffering 539 casualties, including their commanding officer. Staying on the track, just before it meets the Ovillers-Authuille road, to the right and ahead is an area known as The Nab and beyond it Nab Valley. The 8th York and Lancs advanced across this ground on 1st July into withering machine-gun fire. They suffered the fifth highest casualties of any battalion that day – with nearly 600 all ranks killed, wounded and missing. Among them was Lieutenant-Colonel B.L. Maddison, their commanding officer, whose grave is in Blighty Valley Cemetery.

The track now approaches the main road, and where they meet, **turn left** onto the road and go down into Nab Valley. As the road goes uphill

**Men of the 180R in front line trenches opposite Nab Valley.** *Klaus Spath*

out of the valley, the British front line of 1st July was just among the trees in what is the eastern tip of Authuille Wood. There are still signs of trenches. The German lines were beyond the trees in the valley on the right. The 2nd Manchesters were in the line here on that day, and later moved up to attack the Leipzig Redoubt at Thiepval. Following the road, as it gets nearer to Thiepval – the huge memorial is increasingly visible -a green CWGC sign appears on the left. **Follow the grass path** across the fields to the cemetery.

LONSDALE CEMETERY

As Thiepval was not captured until 26th September 1916, and after that was still very much under German bombardment, the battlefields were not cleared until the Spring of 1917. Burial details at that time made a number of cemeteries, two of which they named after the Lonsdale battalion of the Border Regiment which had fought at the Leipzig Redoubt on 1st July 1916. This battalion was raised by the Earl of Lonsdale in September 1914, and was officially the 11th Border Regiment. In the 1st July fighting it lost twenty-six officers and 490 men killed, wounded and missing. Among them was the commanding officer, Lieutenant-Colonel P.W. Machell who was seriously wounded and died some days later in a Casualty Clearing Station at Warloy-Baillon. He is buried in the military cemetery there. Many of his fellow officers and men are here in Lonsdale Cemetery. The original cemetery was therefore known as Lonsdale No 1 and contained ninety-six graves. It is now Plot I, and was substantially enlarged after the war to accommodate 1,515 British and four Australian burials. Of these over half are unknowns. There are Special Memorials to twenty-two British soldiers.

There are many 1st July graves in Lonsdale Cemetery from the fighting around the Leipzig Redoubt and Nab Valley. Perhaps the most visited is that of Sgt James Yuill Turnbull (IV-G-9) of the 17th Highland Light Infantry who won a posthumous Victoria Cross in the Leipzig Redoubt on 1st July. The citation of his award reads:

'For conspicuous bravery and devotion to duty, when, having with his party captured a post apparently of great importance to the enemy, he was subjected to severe counter-attacks, which were continuous throughout the whole day. Although his party was wiped out and replaced several times during the day, Sergeant Turnbull never wavered in his determination to hold the post, the loss of which would have been very serious. Almost single-handed, he maintained his position, and displayed the highest degree of valour and skill in the performance of his duties. Later in the day this very gallant soldier was killed whilst bombing a counter-attack from the parados of our trench.'[4]

'Jimmy' Turnbull was a popular man in his battalion, and before the war had been a keen local footballer in Glasgow. He joined the 17th Highland Light Infantry (Glasgow Commercials) when they were formed in 1914 and was a Sergeant by the end of 1915. An eyewitness account records that Turnbull was, ironically, killed by a German sniper during a lull in the fighting.

Elsewhere in the cemetery is another brave soldier killed in the fighting around the Leipzig

**Sergeant Turnbull VC in action at Leipzig Redoubt.**

Redoubt on 1st July. L/Cpl C.J. Clarke (I-B-18) had been awarded both the DCM and MM, and was killed serving with the 1st Dorsets, Charles Douie's battalion. A young company commander is also buried here, Captain G.Y. Heald (V-E-1) of the 15th Lancashire Fusiliers (1st Salford Pals) who died aged twenty on 1st July. A very young soldier lies in a nearby plot; Pte Thomas Moore (IV-M-6) was only sixteen when he died fighting with the 8th Loyal North Lancs near Thiepval. Young Moore had been in France several months before he was killed.

**Leaving the cemetery** by the grass lane, rejoin the main road and **turn left**, going uphill towards a grouping of trees on the skyline. At the top there is a junction of road and tracks; stop here and look back towards Authuille Wood to your right. The nose of the Leipzig Redoubt was just behind you, and you are now looking down across the ground over which the 17th Highland Light Infantry advanced at zero hour on 1st July 1916. The 11th Border Regiment (Lonsdales) and 1st Dorsets also came up this slope later in the morning, to join the ferocious fighting in the redoubt. The potential field of fire of the German machine-gunners can clearly be seen from this vantage point.

Turning round to look towards the Thiepval memorial, follow the track leading into the trees just ahead of you. The track dips down as you reach the trees, as this is an old quarry. Occasional notices indicate that animal traps abound in the undergrowth, so it is unwise to explore this area. The quarry was at the heart of the Leipzig Redoubt, and to the left of it was a strong position known as The Naze. The 17th Highland Light Infantry came into the quarry on 1st July, and it was near here that Jimmy Turnbull carried out his bombing attacks, earning him a posthumous VC. Despite the heroism of the Highlanders, and later the Lonsdales and Dorsets, this position was not fully taken on 1st July. Some trenches close to the quarry were captured, but the area did not properly fall into British hands until Thiepval was captured in September 1916. **Continue on the track** through the quarry. It runs straight into the grounds of the Thiepval memorial. After passing the memorial's boundary fence stay on the track until it comes out onto a large area covered with stone chippings.

## THIEPVAL MEMORIAL

Thiepval was one of the largest villages on the Somme in 1914. A wealthy family owned a chateau on the western outskirts of the village, which had considerable grounds and buildings. Most of the people who lived in the village were employed at the chateau. After fighting near Thiepval in September 1914, the Germans realised the importance of the village – it stood on high ground and commanded a wide area around. Thiepval was therefore turned into a fortress, with the ruins of the chateau becoming part of the front line. The remaining buildings were destroyed in the preliminary bombardment prior to 1st July, and when the village was finally taken in September 1916 there was virtually nothing to indicate a village had ever been there. During the war the family who once lived in the chateau died with no heirs, and therefore never returned. The land they had owned was partially sold off, but only a handful of pre-war families came back to Thiepval, as with the chateau gone there was no employment.

With the vast number of men missing, and therefore with no known

**The Missing of the Somme: The Thiepval Memorial.**

grave, the then Imperial War Graves Commission planned to erect a number of memorials in France and Belgium so that every fallen soldier would be commemorated in some form. Records showed that around half of the 150,000 British dead on the Somme in 1916 had no known grave, which amounted to tens of thousands of individuals. It was clear that a huge memorial would be required, even bigger than the Menin Gate at Ypres, which by the early 1920s was well in hand. It took a lot longer to finish the Thiepval memorial; in fact the memorial, designed by Sir Edwin Lutyens, was not finished until 1932. It was built on ground that once belonged to the chateau, but not on the actual chateau site. The Thiepval memorial was unveiled later that year, when a huge crowd turned up to see the Prince of Wales and remember husbands, fathers, sons, brothers, cousins and, no doubt, lovers.

Over the years names have been added, records amended; although no names have been taken off the memorial. Today Thiepval commemorates 73,357 soldiers; Army, Royal Naval Division and South African. Other former Empire nations, such as Canada and Australia, are commemorated on their own memorials elsewhere in France. The largest number of names from one regiment is the London Regiment with some 4,348 soldiers. So many names, and so many lives. It is impossible to mention even a fraction of them here. Many people visit the memorial to see the name of a relative, others see the names of their county regiment. A cross section of the type of men commemorated here might therefore include:

THE BATTALION COMMANDER, Major George Sutherland Guyon was a regular army officer with many years service.

93

**Major G.S. Guyon, Royal Fusiliers, killed at Serre commanding the 1st Bradford Pals.**

Born in January 1875, he was educated at Brighton College before joining the Royal Fusiliers. By 1914 he was a Major, and was serving with the 2nd Battalion in Calcutta. The 2nd Royal Fusiliers returned to England, and Guyon later served with them at Gallipoli. He came to France with the battalion in April 1916, and was promoted acting Lieutenant-Colonel and posted to command the 16th West Yorkshire Regiment (1st Bradford Pals). This was a Kitchener's Army battalion and one of several that underwent a change of command prior to the Somme offensive; in each case the original commanding officer was replaced with a Regular or Indian Army officer. The reaction Guyon got when he joined the Bradford Pals is not recorded, but he was one of twenty-two officer casualties suffered by the battalion in the fighting at Serre on 1st July 1916. His name appears on the Royal Fusiliers panel, where his substantive rank of Major is shown.

THE YOUNG SOLDIER, Pte Reginald Giles is the youngest soldier recorded in the Thiepval memorial registers; Giles was only fourteen years old when he was killed west of High Wood with the Gloucestershire Regiment on 20th August 1916. Born in Cirencester, he enlisted in Birmingham but his parents resided at 30 Lewis Lane, Cirencester, Gloucestershire. Reginald Giles was one of the youngest soldiers to fall in the Battle of the Somme. His name can be found on the Gloucestershire Regiment panel.

THE POET, Lieutenant Thomas Michael Kettle is one of the best known Irish poets of the Great War. Born at Artane, County Dublin, in February 1880, Tom Kettle was educated at University College, Dublin. James Joyce was one of Kettle's contemporaries at university. He gained a reputation as a good public speaker, and became heavily involved in Irish Nationalist politics. Kettle practised law after finishing his education, and stood for parliament in 1906 winning the East Tyrone seat. He married in 1909, and continued to be at the centre of Nationalist politics until 1910. He supported the Home Rule Bill in 1912, and was actively engaged in the Irish Volunteer movement prior to 1914. Commissioned in the Royal Dublin Fusiliers, Tom Kettle served abroad with the 9th Battalion in the 16th (Irish) Division. Serving first in the Loos sector, he was killed commanding his company at Ginchy on 9th September 1916, and although he originally had a grave it was lost in later fighting. Tom Kettle's poem *Paddy*, in which he mimics Kipling's *Tommy*, remains an example of some of his finest work; it ends by saying the Irish Division would be in the firing line '... when the Price of God is paid'. Tom Kettle paid that price in full. His name can be found on the Royal Dublin Fusiliers panel.

THE WRITER: Hector Hugo Munro was better known by his pen name of 'Saki' and is widely acknowledged as one of the best British short story writers of the twentieth century. Munro was born in Burma in 1870, but was brought up in Devon. He started his writing career on the Westminster Gazette, and later worked as a foreign corespondent for the *Morning Post* in the Balkans, Paris and Russia. He published his first collection of short stories in 1904, and later went on to write three novels and three plays. When war came in August 1914, Munro joined the 22nd Battalion Royal Fusiliers (Kensingtons) as a Private soldier, and fought with them on the Western Front from 1915. He constantly refused a commission, but rose to the rank of Sergeant. Munro was killed by the explosion of a shell on Redan ridge, 14th November 1916, aged forty-six. His name can be found on the Royal Fusiliers panel.

THE COMPOSER, Lieutenant George Sainton Kaye Butterworth MC was a British composer and musician of some note, known in particular for his musical interpretations of A.E. Housman's poetry, *A Shropshire Lad*. Butterworth joined the Durham Light Infantry and was serving with the 13th Battalion by the Somme. He was awarded the Military Cross for bravery near Munster Alley, near Pozieres, in July 1916. At the time a new trench was named after him; Butterworth Trench. He and his unit returned to Munster Alley a month later, and George Butterworth was killed near the trench that bore his surname on 5th August 1916. His name can be found on the Durham Light Infantry panel.

## THIEPVAL ANGLO-FRENCH CEMETERY

This cemetery is located to the rear of the Thiepval memorial, and contains an equal number of British and French burials to symbolise the joint effort of the Anglo-French forces on the Somme in 1916. The vast majority of the 300 Tommies and 300 Poilus in this cemetery are unknowns; the British burials were all isolated graves found in the early 1930s. They come from a wide area on the Somme battlefield, and several from as far away as Loos and Arras.

**Leave the memorial grounds via the car park**, which is located on the left as you come away from the memorial. Once in the car park, **turn left down** a straight road lined by woodland on either side. A memorial can be seen at the end; **follow the road to the memorial**. This is a memorial to the 18th (Eastern) Division. The 18th was a Kitchener's Army division composed of regiments from South-East England. It was very much a Somme Division, arriving in the sector in the Summer of 1915. Regarded as among the finest fighting formations on the Western Front, the 18th was one of the few divisions to achieve all its objectives on 1st July, fought gallantly at the capture of Trones Wood and was the only division to assault and capture Thiepval; the village fell to units of the 18th on 26th September 1916. After the war the division's Old Comrades Association erected a number of permanent memorials on the old battlefields: two were on the Somme – one here and the other at Trones Wood.

There are superb views towards Thiepval Wood. The German front line on the outskirts of Thiepval lay very close to this memorial, and the chateau was on the site of the farm buildings to your right. The British lines were down the slope in front of the wood. On 1st July the 15th Lancashire Fusiliers (1st Salford Pals) advanced up this ground; by the end of the day there were only three officers and 150 men left in the battalion which had attacked that morning. From the memorial continue along the main road (D.151) into Thiepval village, and the church. A farm is passed on the left, continue on and past the church on your right until you reach a cross-roads in the village. **Turn left** on the

**Thiepval Chateau as it appeared in the years before the war.**

96

D.73 going downhill on a steep banked road. Stay on this until Connaught Cemetery is reached on the left.

## CONNAUGHT CEMETERY, THIEPVAL

This cemetery is located just in front of the former British first line trenches of 1st July. The 10th Inniskillings, and the 8th and 14th Royal Irish Rifles advanced across this ground after zero hour. The German lines were near to the location of Mill Road Cemetery, which can clearly be seen from where you are. Connaught Cemetery was opened in the late autumn of 1916, as the Ancre Heights fighting moved on towards Grandcourt. By the end of the war there were 228 graves here, which now form Plot I. Enlarged after 1918, the cemetery now has 1,278 British burials; among them 642 unknowns. There are seven Special Memorials.

The graves reflect the heavy losses suffered by both the 36th (Ulster) and 49th (West Riding) Divisions in the fighting at Thiepval. Among the more interesting individuals are Lieutenant A.M. Hopkins (VIII-E-10) who came from a very political family; his father was an M.P. and his mother a senior member of the London County Council. He was killed in action aged only eighteen on 18th November 1916. A long serving officer was Captain W. Newcombe (XII-M-4) who died whilst attached to the 8th South Lancs on 3rd July 1916, aged forty-four. His

**Connaught Cemetery in 1919. All that is left of Thiepval Wood are a few tree stumps.**

grave bears the rare badge of the 1st Royal Dragoons, and he had previously served over twenty three years in the Royal Horse Guards.

Leaving the cemetery go back onto the road. A green CWGC sign points up a **grass lane** towards Mill Road Cemetery. **Follow this**.

MILL ROAD CEMETERY

Located close to the German front line of 1st July, you have just walked the attack route from the British positions near Thiepval Wood. The main objective of the advance was the Schwaben Redoubt, a large defensive position in the German support lines. The area where the Redoubt was can be seen from the back of the cemetery – on ground in front of a large farm to the north-east of the cemetery. The graves are 1,304 in number, with six Special Memorials – some 815 of the total number are unknowns. Although there are many Ulster Division burials, men from a number of Yorkshire regiments are just as numerous. The original graves in Plot I were enlarged after the war, when burials from all over the Ancre and Thiepval battlefields were concentrated into the cemetery. In the centre many graves are laid flat; unique on the Somme. The reason is that below Mill Road Cemetery the many tunnels and dugouts of the German trench system still remain and movement over the years has made the ground unstable. Another young soldier is buried here; William John Andrews (I-D-4) was only seventeen when he died with the 7th Bedfordshires at Thiepval on 28th September 1916 - just a boy, but the register records he was a Corporal. Elsewhere are two early pioneers of the tank: Lieutenant H.W. Hitchcock (II-B-10) of A Battalion Heavy Branch Machine Gun Corps died near St Pierre Divion on 13th November 1916; buried beside him is one of his crew, Gnr W.J. Miles (II-B-9).

**Return to the main road** by the grass lane, and **turn right** following the road to the nearby Ulster Tower. The Ulster Tower is a copy of Helen's Tower at Clandeboyne near Belfast, where some units of the 36th Division trained in 1914. It was erected after the war as a memorial to the thousands of men from the division who died on the Western Front, and in particular those who died at Thiepval on 1st July 1916. It is located on the site of the front line trench attacked by the 9th Royal Irish Rifles, and for many years entry to the memorial was only possible by obtaining a key from the keeper in Hamel. The Tower is now owned by the Somme Association; sadly access to the top of the memorial is prohibited, but a room containing plaques and wreaths may still be seen at the bottom. To the rear of the Ulster Tower new buildings house a visitor's centre, tea room and good toilets. This is open every day, except Sundays and Mondays, and is staffed by local French people who speak little or no English. A slide show about the Ulster Division and a small display of artefacts are also worth a look. In and around the grounds are a number of new memorials; one commemorates the Victoria Cross winners of the division, while a more recent one outside the main gate is in memory of the men and women of the Orange Order who died in all twentieth century conflicts.

**Return to the main road**. A diversion can be made here by taking a **track to the right**, between the Orangemen memorial and the outside wall of the Ulster Tower grounds. This track leads you down hill until the remains of a German concrete emplacement are seen on the right of the track. This emplacement, probably an observation post, was in a German salient position known to the Ulstermen as The Pope's Nose. The 15th Royal Irish Rifles and 1/6th West Yorkshires attacked the trenches here on 1st July. There are commanding views towards the British lines which were on the edge of Thiepval Wood. Further views across the valley take in Hamel village, the Newfoundland Park on the skyline and Ancre British cemetery; the white, almost ghostlike traces of old trenches are often visible in fields to the right of this cemetery.

**Ulster Tower memorial.**

**Return to the main road** via the track, and **turn right** past the Orangemen memorial. The road goes down into the valley, with Thiepval Wood on the left. At the bottom of the hill a road appears on the right, sign-posted C.7 to St Pierre-Divion. Directly opposite on the left is a cart track that winds back towards Thiepval Wood. Follow this track; further along, as it turns a corner, the track is wooded on both sides. From here onwards there are steep wooded banks on the left hand side. The marshes of the Ancre can be seen among the trees to the right. This is the rear of Thiepval Wood as far as the British lines were concerned. During the Battle of the Somme there were many dugouts and dumps in these banks. Whole battalions were bivouaced here at a time, and there are many undulations visible between the trees. Thiepval Wood is strictly private, and should not be entered.

After some time, the track eventually reaches a fork; **take the right hand fork** into an open area of ground, near a campsite. Continue along the track, which is in a much better condition for this part of the route. At a minor junction the track becomes a metalled road, and opens up into fields again. Dead ahead on the horizon are the trees of the Leipzig

Redoubt. As you emerge from the trees a small valley opens up on the left. The wooded area was known as Caterpillar Wood and beyond it the Salford Pals and 16th Northumberland Fusiliers assembled for the attack on Thiepval. Communication trenches ran in these fields, leading to the front line below the village. The Thiepval memorial can clearly be seen, as well as the distinctive 18th Division obelisk.

**Continue along the road**, past an old shack on the left. At the top the road joins the main Thiepval-Authuille road (D.151). **Turn right** for Authuille the outskirts of which are reached after only about fifty yards or so. **Continue back into the village**. As you reach the village war memorial on the left, stop to view the recently erected memorial to the Salford Pals. This was placed here by members of the Lancashire and Cheshire Branch of the Western Front Association on 1st July 1995. In the main square in front of the church, a road (Rue D'en Bas) runs to the right of the church and leads you back to Authuille Military Cemetery and your vehicle.

### READING LIST

Coppard, G.    *With A Machine Gun to Cambrai* (Imperial War Museum 1969)
Crozier, F.P.    *A Brass Hat In No Man's Land* (Cape 1930)
Douie, C.    *The Weary Road* (Murray 1929)
Mitchell, G.S. *Three Cheers for the Derrys! A History of the 10th Royal Inniskilling Fusiliers* (Yes! 1991)
Orr, P.    *The Road to the Somme* (Blackstaff Press 1987)
Shepherd, E.    *A Sergeant Major's War*
Stedman, M. *The Salford Pals* (Pen & Sword 1993)
Stedman, M. *Battleground Europe*: Thiepval (Pen & Sword 1995)

**Men of the Border Regiment resting in 'funk holes' in Thiepval Wood.**

# THE AIF – POZIÈRES BATTLEFIELD WALK

STARTING POINT: **Ovillers church**
DURATION: **3 ½ hours**
WALK SUMMARY: **Staring from the positions in Ovillers reached by British troops in mid-July 1916, the walk focuses on the early attacks on German defences around Pozières village and fighting through July-August-September when units of the Australian Imperial Force (AIF) were heavily engaged.**

*Ovillers church is in the centre of the village, on the minor road that runs through it. There is good off-road parking in front and to the side of the church. Leaving the vehicle, go east in the direction of Pozières to the outskirts of the village and past the water tower on the right. Ahead of you is a blue and white modern farm building; walk to it as the road forks. Take the left hand fork – effectively going straight on – and go past the blue and white farm buildings, now on your right. Just past the main barn, stop; to the right is a panoramic view towards Pozières.*

Ovillers had been a 1st July objective but was not captured until 17th July when units of the 48th (South Midland) Division finally pushed the remains of the German garrison out of the village. Trench lines then stabilised east of the village towards Pozières – the next objective. Pozières was a heavily fortified village in the German second line of

**The ruins of Ovillers, July 1916.**

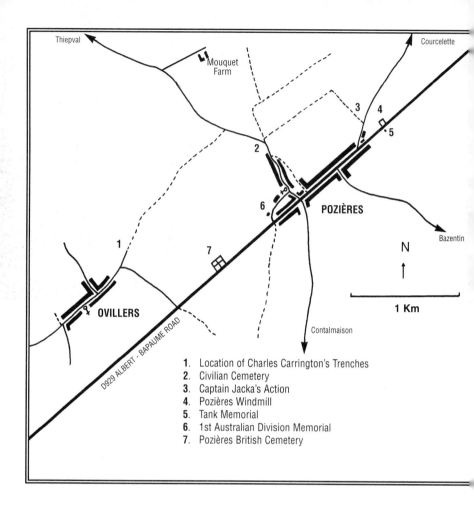

1. Location of Charles Carrington's Trenches
2. Civilian Cemetery
3. Captain Jacka's Action
4. Pozières Windmill
5. Tank Memorial
6. 1st Australian Division Memorial
7. Pozières British Cemetery

defences. On some of the highest ground on the Somme battlefield, German positions in and around the village had commanding views of the ground before them – particularly towards Ovillers, where the new trench lines settled down after the capture of that village. Machine-gun positions existed all round the village, with a huge concrete pillbox on the western outskirts of Pozières astride the Albert-Bapaume Road and known on British maps as Gibralter. East of the village was the ruins of an old windmill, reinforced by the Germans as an observation post with deep dugouts below it. Thick belts of wire screened the approaches to the village, and well dug in German artillery batteries back towards Courcelette commanded No Man's Land. The main German lines here were known to the British as OG1 and OG2, Old German lines 1 and 2.

The first major advance on Pozières began on 23rd July 1916 when

**Men of the AIF before moving up to Pozières.**

the 48th (South Midland) and 1st (Australian) Divisions attacked the village following a four day bombardment; the 48th advanced north of the Bapaume road and 1st (Australian) came up from the south. The ground before you from this vantage point looks across the area advanced over by the 145th Brigade of the 48th Division on that day. From left to right the attacking battalions were: 1/5th Gloucestershire Regiment, 1/4th Oxs and Bucks Light Infantry and 1/4th Royal Berkshires. The 1/1st Bucks Battalion was in reserve. Trenches south of the road you are on now were taken by 12.30am, but German counter-attacks from north of Ovillers prevented any further advance here, despite the fact that the Bucks Battalion was brought in to the fight. To the south of Pozières, the 1st (Australian) Division had fared much better. The trench system there was captured and an entry into the village forced by the early hours of 24th July. The OG lines were also entered by men of the 3rd Australian Brigade, despite a strong German counter-attack.

Just past this vantage point by the farm, to the left of the track you are on ground where Great War author Charles Carrington, an officer in the Royal Warwickshire Regiment of 48th Division, had a post and where his battalion beat off several German counter-attacks from the direction of Pozières. The Warwicks had advanced from the Albert-Bapaume road towards this position and Carrington left this vivid description of the attack:

'I found myself now in a long slope of rough grass, knee high

**Charles Carrington**

and tangled, in sight, after all, of what looked like the battalion... on our right the line went forward... we went on in the dark, breaking now and then into the double. The exhilaration of that rush of men was wonderful... the bayonets gleamed in the flashes of the barrage that crashed in front of us.'[1]

Carrington's men, however, advanced no further than the site of this post and a good account of the subsequent fighting can be found in his book *A Subaltern's War*, published in 1929 under the pseudonym of Charles Edmonds.

**Continue along the road**, which after a while loses its metalled surface and becomes a track. A second vantage point is reached further on. From here there is a good view across the valley in front of Pozières. On the high ground ahead the traffic on the Albert-Bapaume road can be clearly seen, along with the high walls of the Pozières British Cemetery. To the left there is another good view of the village; the pointed memorial to the 1st (Australian) Division is visible on the outskirts near where the Gibralter pillbox once stood. The radio aerial near the site of Pozières Windmill is visible rising above the roof tops.

After the initial advance heavy fighting took place in the northern end of the village when the 4th and 8th Battalions AIF came up through the ruins of Pozières from the Bapaume Road on 25th July. They engaged the German defenders in an area just north-west of the village – visible from where you are now – around a position known as K Trench. This was a deep trench with a barricade at one end behind which the Germans were waiting for the 4th Battalion. A heavy bombing match followed, but Australian bombers were given covering fire by the 4th's Lewis gunners and good progress was made. Meanwhile, the 8th Battalion advanced in extended order through the village. In the midst of their attack, their Lewis gunners were also proving indispensable. Among them was Private Thomas Cooke. Cooke was a thirty-five year old New Zealander who had emigrated to Australian in 1912. He joined the AIF in 1915, serving at Gallipoli, then Egypt and finally in France with the 7th Battalion. He transferred to the 8th prior to the Somme, and in the fighting at Poziè ßfres:

> '... he was ordered to take his gun and gun-team to a dangerous part of the line. Here he did fine work, but came under very heavy fire, with the result that he was the only man left. He was still stuck to his post and continued to fire his gun. When assistance was sent he was found dead beside his gun. He set a splendid

106

example of determination and devotion to duty.'[2]
For his bravery that day Cooke was awarded a posthumous Victoria Cross. he was one of nearly 400 casualties in the 8th Battalion. After the war his grave could not be found and today he is commemorated on the Villers-Bretonneux Memorial.

**Continue along the track**; it eventually reaches the main Pozières-Thiepval road (D.73). The Thiepval Memorial is clearly visible on the horizon to the left. **Now turn right** onto the main road and follow in the direction of Pozières. After a few hundred yards the road bends to the right. The village cemetery, near where Thomas Cooke was killed and won his VC, can be seen on the right. A clump of trees is situated on the bend to the left, and there are often many live shells left in the verge. On the bend itself **turn left** in front of the clump of trees; two minor roads are immediately visible – take the right hand one running north-east towards Courcelette. At the start of the track there is a good vantage point looking towards the former site of Pozières Windmill. From here the ground east of the village can be seen. Pozières was in Australian hands by 26th July, but the fighting cost the 1st (Australian) Division some 5,285 casualties, the 1st Brigade alone losing nearly 2,000 men. They were relieved by units of the 2nd (Australian) Division and moved back to billets around Vadencourt Wood. The 2nd Division occupied the new lines east of the village in preparation for the next advance across the Pozières Heights which lay ahead of them. The German OG lines ran roughly from the site of Pozières Windmill; from where you are the former position of the windmill is opposite the large radio aerial on the Albert-Bapaume road. The twin flag poles of the Australian memorial are clearly visible. Further attacks by the 2nd Division began on 29th July, but although OG1 and OG2 were entered, the fighting proved inconclusive. Charles Bean, the AIF's historian, recorded that:

'... the hail of bullets was such as had not been experienced in the AIF since the fighting of 8th May 1915 at Cape Helles [Gallipoli].'[3]

The lines settled down for a few days whilst the intense German bombardment that swept the Pozières battlefield continued.

Now continue along the minor road; after a while it becomes a cart track. As Courcelette becomes visible ahead on the skyline, the track turns to the right – follow it. After a few hundred yards the track joins the main Courcelette-Pozières road. Stop. It was near the junction of track and road that on 7th August 1916 Albert Jacka VC took part in one of the most noted acts of gallantry in the Pozières fighting. A German counter-attack had been launched on the Australian lines

**A modern aerial view of Pozières from above the eastern edge of the village looking towards Ovillers.**   *John Giles*

running north-west from the windmill. Among the Australian units was the 14th Battalion commonly known in the AIF as 'Jacka's Mob' after Lieutenant Albert Jacka, an officer in the unit. Jacka was the first man in the AIF to win the Victoria Cross, as a Sergeant in the 14th at Gallipoli in 1915. He was subsequently commissioned, and like many AIF soldiers was never afraid to venture an opinion over operations he thought to be unwise or which were being handled incorrectly. It made him an unpopular figure in certain circles.

On 7th August, Jacka and his comrades of the 14th Battalion were in some old dugouts in the OG line near the Pozières Windmill when a large explosion disturbed their sleep; German troops were at the entrance to Jacka's dugout and had lobbed down a bomb. Jacka returned with two shots from his revolver and:

'... rushed up, followed by his men, who had to scramble over two of their groaning mates, maimed by the bomb. The enemy had swept past and could be seen in large numbers between this dugout and the village of Pozières. Jacka instantly decided to line up all the sound men he could find, seven or eight in number, and to dash through the enemy... his men had hardly been drawn up when he saw the column of 48th Battalion's prisoners and their escort returning towards him. He let them come to within thirty yards and then jumped out of the back of the trench and charged. About half the German guards threw down their rifles, but the rest opened fire, and every man of Jacka's small party was hit with rifle bullets.'[4]

The 48th Battalion prisoners joined in, and,

'... the fight immediately became a melee, into the thick of which Jacka and the survivors of his small party plunged... the Germans included a number of bombers, and some were fighting from shell-holes. Jacka dived in among them, killing and capturing a number, but receiving a wound that nearly killed him.'[5]

Jacka was eventually evacuated down the line with this and several other wounds sustained in the fighting. The counter-attack was held, and the front of the 14th and 48th Battalions saved – largely by Jacka's

**Captain Albert Jacka VC MC (left) shaking the hand of Private O'Meara, who won the VC at Pozières. Jacka was then convalescing after the numerous wounds he received opposite Pozières Windmill.**

act. Indeed, Bean felt it '... the most dramatic and effective act of individual audacity in the history of the A.I.F.'[6]. Jacka was recommended for a bar to his Victoria Cross, but the award was never granted; he received the Military Cross instead. Many in the AIF felt great bitterness over this – that Jacka, an often unpopular figure among senior officers, had been robbed of his medal. But this was not Albert Jacka's last action; he went on to serve with the 14th Battalion at Bullecourt in May 1917, where he was awarded a bar to his Military Cross.

**Turn right** at the track/road junction towards Pozières. Where the road joins the main Albert-Bapaume road (D.929) **turn left**. This road is often busy, with large lorries thundering by. A large grass verge is

**Pozières Windmill in ruins, 1916.**

sited on both sides of the road and it is easier to walk on this. The Pozières Windmill site is reached a few hundred yards further up on the left (north) side of the road. Pozières Windmill was situated on the highest ground around the village, indeed some of the highest on the 1916 Somme battlefield. It was partially in ruins by July 1916, and by the time the Australian attack of 4th August 1916 reached here it was just a pile of rubble. However, the Germans had reinforced both it and the cellars with concrete, and turned the site into a heavily fortified position. On 4th August, the 27th Battalion AIF and 7th Company Australian Machine Gun Corps attacked along the route you have just walked, advancing on the windmill. They suffered heavy casualties, but established a foothold near the ruins. Then the Vickers machine-guns of 7th Company, commanded by Lieutenant Percy Cherry, fought off counter-attack after counter-attack; Cherry was awarded the Military Cross for his bravery here that day. He went on to win a posthumous VC at Lagnicourt in March 1917. On 5th August, a small party of the 28th Battalion under Captain Cecil Maitland Foss entered the area of the windmill, and finally captured it – during the action Foss was badly wounded and died of these wounds at a Casualty Clearing Station at Puchevillers on 11th August[7].

Fighting continued in the ground visible from the windmill until early September 1916, when the Australians were relieved and Canadian troops entered the lines which had now moved nearer to Courcelette. As the memorial on the site of Pozières Windmill states:

'... here was the centre of the struggle in this part of the Somme Battlefield in July and August 1916... Australian troops fell more thickly on this ridge than on any other battlefield of the war.'

Indeed the fighting at Pozières had cost the AIF some 23,000 casualties.

Today there are fine views across the battlefield from the mound of the windmill. Thiepval, the Ancre Heights and Courcelette are all visible on a clear day. Concrete blocks from when the Germans reinforced the position can be seen among the grass and a newly erected bronze orientation table gives further information to visitors. Opposite the windmill site is another memorial – to the Tank Corps. After the Canadians took over the sector at Pozières a further advance was made on 15th September 1916 during the Battle of Flers-Courcelette. It was during these operations that tanks were used for the first time- with mixed results. The tanks involved in the Courcelette attack formed up on the site of the current memorial, and it was their rallying point to return to after the action. It was therefore considered a suitable location for the only memorial to the Tank Corps in France and Belgium. The memorial itself is bordered by six-pounder gun barrels linked with driving chain, and is flanked by four superb bronze models of different types of tank. One has bullet damage from 1944 when a German convoy was strafed by an American Lightening aircraft.

Leave the Tank Memorial and **return along the Bapaume road** – keeping to the grass verge – back into Pozières. The village is roughly the size it was prior to the Great War and now boasts two bars. One is passed on the way into the centre of the village; the other, containing a museum, can be visited later on. In the middle of Pozières **turn right** at the D.73 junction signposted to the Thiepval Memorial and Newfoundland Park, up the Rue d l'Eglise. After about a hundred yards a further road to the left is seen. On the corner is the old Cafe de la Mairie (now closed) and opposite it on the other side of the turning is

**The main street of Pozières looking towards Bapaume, August 1914.**

**The 1st Australian Division memorial flanked by two German 77mm field guns.**

Pozières church; inside is an Australian flag, but the church is rarely open, except on and around ANZAC Day, 25th April.

**Turn left** down this road, the continuation of Rue de l'Eglise. Past some modern houses on the right the 1st (Australian) Division Memorial is reached on a bend in the road. This memorial commemorates the 5,285 men of the division who became casualties at Pozières. It also records the battle honours awarded to the division in later battles of the war. At one time two German 77mm field guns flanked the obelisk, but these apparently disappeared during the Second World War. Another bronze orientation table – similar to the one at Pozières Windmill – is situated by the entrance to the memorial. There are good views from the rear of this memorial, looking back over the valley west of Pozières where you were walking earlier and where the 48th (South Midland) Division advanced in July 1916. The advantage German observers had is clearly seen here.

Up a bank among the trees, almost opposite the memorial, is the former site of the Gibralter Pillbox. This huge construction was destroyed in later fighting, but the dugouts beneath it survived and the entrance to one was uncovered in 1986. In the Spring of 1994 further excavations were made by the Historial at Peronne, and a large chamber opened up. Two years later in 1996 further work cleared the main dugout and the site has been wired up until proper public access can be completed. From Gibralter **continue along the minor road** until it reaches the main Albert-Bapaume road (D.929). A detour to the second cafe in the village is made by **turning left** and following the pavement for a couple of hundred yards. Known locally as Pozières Cafe, or the 'Burma Star Cafe', it serves lunches as well as liquid refreshment. Inside there is a good display of battlefield relics, many for sale. Otherwise **turn right** at this junction onto the main road, following the verge to Pozières British Cemetery clearly seen further on.

## POZIERES BRITISH CEMETERY

This large and impressive cemetery began as a burial ground used by fighting units and Field Ambulances around an area known in 1916 as Tramway Crossing or Red Cross Corner. These original burials are today in Plot II, the plot to the right of the main entrance as you walk into the cemetery. Other graves were brought in from a wide area around Pozières and Ovillers after the war and among them were graves from Casualty Corner Cemetery near Contalmaison, which included twenty-one AIF graves from the Pozières fighting. There are now 1,809 British burials, 690 Australian, 218 Canadian and sixteen whose unit is not known. Of these 1,374 are unknown. In addition,

**Pozières British Military Cemetery in 1919; the large white cross commemorated men of the 8th Bn AIF.**

there are twenty-two Special Memorials to men known to be buried in the cemetery.

It reflects well the fighting around Pozières; with graves from units in the 48th Division who attacked in July 1916, as well as many AIF men killed in the fighting in and around the village. A number of 8th Battalion men are buried here; comrades of Private Thomas Cooke VC. Perhaps his unknown grave is among them? One VC winner is certainly buried in the cemetery; Sergeant Claude Charles Castleton (IV-L-43). Castleton served with the 5th Company Australian Machine Gun Corps and received a posthumous award on 29th July 1916 in fighting south of the village. His citation reads:

> 'For most conspicuous bravery. During an   attack on the enemy's trenches the infantry  was temporarily driven back by the intense  machine-gun fire opened by the enemy. Many wounded were left in No Man's Land lying in  shell holes. Serjt Castleton went out twice in face of this intense fire and each time  brought in a wounded man on his back. He went out a third time and was bringing in another  wounded man when he was himself hit in the back and killed instantly. He set a splendid example of courage and self-sacrifice.'[8]

Castleton was twenty-three when he was killed, and was from Lowestoft in Suffolk. He emigrated to Australia in 1912, working on a sheep farm and then travelled extensively throughout Australia. On the outbreak of war he was in Papua New Guinea and after enlisting served at Gallipoli with the 18th Battalion before transferring to the Australian Machine Gun Corps in 1916.

Another brave Digger buried in the cemetery is Major Murdock Mackay (III-E-7). He was killed with the 22nd Battalion on 4th August 1916, just short of OG1. Charles Bean, the AIF historian, left this description of him in the thick of the Pozières fighting:

> '... Mackay was doing the work of ten, collecting disjointed parties, directing,   leading, driving... on reaching the trench, without waiting for consultation, he assumed control and calling 'Come on boys!', instantly  led the troops forward.'[9]

Before the war Mackay had attended Melbourne University, where he studied Law, and became a barrister by the age of twenty-one. His difficult temperament in dealing with his superiors – a common trait beloved of the AIF – had often got him into trouble and at one time almost prevented his promotion to the rank of Major. However, at the fighting around Pozières his stubbornness proved decisive in saving the situation – and the lives of many of his men at the cost of his own.

The walls that surround the cemetery form the panels of the Pozières

Memorial to the Missing. This memorial commemorates the men of Gough's Fifth Army who died in the German Spring Offensive in March 1918. There are 14,644 names on it, which like most memorials to the missing are in Corps and Regimental order. It was originally intended that this memorial would be erected near St Quentin – the sector where most of the men commemorated here died – but by the time of construction the French were becoming anxious about the amount of ground being given up to British cemeteries and memorials. For a reason which remains unknown, Pozières British Cemetery was selected as the new location; strange, as this part of the Somme was in Third Army sector in March 1918.

Leaving the cemetery **turn right** and return to the main road going in the direction of La Boisselle and Albert. Stay on the verge until a minor road to the right appears; follow the sign to Ovillers and take the road back into the village and church where your vehicle is parked.

READING LIST:

Bean, C.E.W.  *The AIF In France Volume III:1916* (Sydney 1929)
Charlton, P.  *Pozières: Australians on the Somme* (Leo Cooper 1986)
Edmonds, C.  *A Subaltern's War* (Peter Davies 1929)
Laffin, J.  *Guide to the Australian Battlefields of the Western Front 1916-1918* (Kangaroo Press 1992)

# THE YORKSHIRE WALK: FRICOURT
## 1ST JULY 1916

STARTING POINT: **Norfolk Cemetery, Becourt**
DURATION: **3 hours**
WALK SUMMARY: **This walk focuses on a number of Yorkshire Battalions, all of whom fought at Fricourt on 1st July 1916: 9th King's Own Yorkshire Light Infantry, 7th and 10th Yorkshires, 7th East Yorkshires and 10th West Yorkshires. It is very much an off the road walk, using tracks which give commanding views across the Fricourt battlefield.**

*Park your vehicle outside Norfolk Cemetery; there is plenty of room to pull right off the road. Visit the cemetery before leaving.*

NORFOLK CEMETERY

This is an early Somme cemetery begun in August 1915 by the 1st Norfolks who were holding the line in this sector at that time. The cemetery was used right through to August 1916, and after the war was expanded by the addition of 268 graves from the Fricourt area. Today there are 407 British graves, nine Australian, three South African, two Canadian, one New Zealand, one Indian; of these 226 are unknowns. Among the early graves are a large number of Royal Engineers Tunnelling Company men who died in mining operations opposite Fricourt. The 178th Tunnelling Company is particularly well represented; they were the unit who worked the Tambour Mines which will be seen later in the walk. An early 178th Company grave is that of Lieutenant W.R. Cloutman (I-A-14) who died on 21st August 1915 while, the register records, '... rescuing a sergeant whom he carried on his shoulder 45 feet up a ladder.' Cloutman was overcome by fumes and died of gas poisoning. A senior officer of the unit who was killed up near Fricourt on 2nd July was Captain A.S. Brothers, aged thirty-four (I-A-86).

The Yorkshire battalions covered during this walk are well represented in this cemetery, in particular the officers of the 9th King's Own Yorkshire Light Infantry (KOYLI). More of their story will be related later, but their graves can be found in Plot I, Row B: which includes the battalion's commanding officer Lieutenant-Colonel C.W.D. Lynch DSO (I-B-87). Lynch was a thirty-five year old former regular officer from a military family – his father was a Major-General

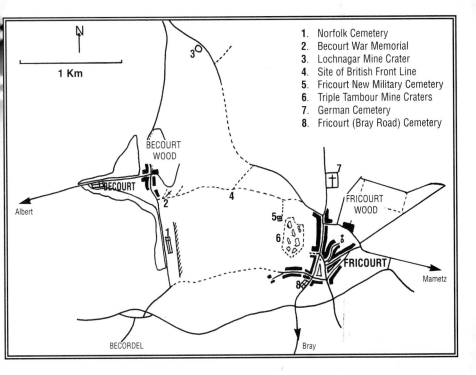

1. Norfolk Cemetery
2. Becourt War Memorial
3. Lochnagar Mine Crater
4. Site of British Front Line
5. Fricourt New Military Cemetery
6. Triple Tambour Mine Craters
7. German Cemetery
8. Fricourt (Bray Road) Cemetery

– who had served with the Duke of Cornwall's Light Infantry in the Boer War. On the reserve of officers in 1914, he was promoted to command 9th KOYLI in June 1915. Awarded the Distinguished Service Order at Loos in September 1915, Lynch was reputedly an unpopular officer in his battalion. However, he died at the head of his men opposite Fricourt on 1st July, along with all four of his company commanders; three of them are buried near him – Captains G. Haswell, L.D. Head and W. Walker. Another important grave is that of Major Stewart Walter Loudoun-Shand (I-C-77) of the 10th Yorkshires; he was awarded a posthumous Victoria Cross for his bravery at Fricourt. Details of his VC action will also be examined later in the walk.

**The grave of Major S W Loudoun-Shand VC in Norfolk Cemetery.**

Leaving the cemetery **turn right** onto the road in the direction of Becourt. Further up, as the outskirts of the village are reached, the road bends and on a corner a cart track is seen going off to the left uphill. On this corner, among the trees on the right, is a crucifix. Set back among the trees and sometimes out of view during the leafy summer months, this is the local Becourt war memorial. It commemorates in particular Lieutenant Joseph de Valincourt, a French officer killed in the Champagne fighting of 1917 whose parents once lived in Becourt Chateau. The **cart track** by the crucifix, sloping off over the high ground, **should now be followed**. Ignoring a branch of the track going off to the left, **continue straight on**. As you go further along the track features to the left and right will become more visible. Becourt Wood is over to your left; the chalk spoil from the Lochnagar mine at La Boisselle was brought here for disposal – the scrub that now marks the site of the Lochnagar Crater will eventually become visible at about 11 o'clock from the track you are on. This mine was blown on 1st July when 60,000lbs of ammonal exploded under the German positions in Sausage Valley. Today the site is owned by Richard Dunning, who bought the crater in 1979 and organises a ceremony there every 1st July. The ground to to the left and right was an area of British communication trenches and reserve positions; further over on the right was a position known as Queen's Redoubt where Major Loudoun-Shand's 10th Yorkshires were in support before moving up to the main attack.

After some distance along this track a junction will be reached at the site of a small clump of trees and scrub. The track to the left goes off down to La Boisselle and the Lochnagar Crater, whilst straight on is Fricourt. There are commanding views from this point, and it is ideal for viewing the Fricourt battlefield in its historical context. The assault on Fricourt was entrusted to elements of two New Army divisions; the 17th (Northern) and 21st. Both had seen action in the earlier fighting of the war; the 17th at Ypres in 1915, and the 21st at Loos in September of the same year. The 21st had achieved a poor reputation after a disastrous attack on Hill 70 when they and another division fell back after terrible losses. This time the division was determined to set the record straight.

The track you are on was used as the dividing line between the 63rd and 64th Brigades of the 21st Division; in fact the trees and scrub are almost exactly on the British front line of 1st July 1916. The 64th Brigade on the left contained the 9th KOYLI. Prior to moving up the line, the officers of this battalion, commanded by the unpopular Lieutenant-Colonel Lynch, had met in the mess for a toast to the

**Officers of 9th KOYLI at La Neuville, Corbie, April 1916. Fifth from the left, front row, is Lieutenant-Colonel C W D Lynch DSO. Captain Gordon Haswell, who proposed the 'When the barrage lifts' toast is front row, third from left.**

regiment. The toast also included the commanding officer's name, but many of those present refused to take part. However, Captain Gordon Haswell, commanding B Company, stepped forward to save the situation by proposing,

> '... Gentlemen, I give you the toast of the King's Own Yorkshire Light Infantry, and in particular the 9th Battalion of the Regiment... Gentlemen, when the barrage lifts...'[1]

When the barrage did lift on 1st July, the 9th KOYLI left their trenches and came under heavy fire in No Man's Land. Lieutenant-Colonel Lynch was killed by the fall of a shell whilst leading his men forward. All four company commanders were also killed, among them Captain Haswell who had proposed the toast. The Scout Officer, Second Lieutenant E.R. Nott was badly wounded, later dying of them at a Base Hospital; the Bombing Officer was wounded, and the Signals Officer was killed. In A Company alone all five officers became casualties-four of the five being killed in action. The total of dead, wounded and missing in 9th KOYLI amounted to 455; the battalion which had left its trenches earlier that morning had all but ceased to exist.

The ground to your immediate right was the area of trenches from which the 10th Yorkshires advanced on 1st July. Initially they had been in reserve near Queen's Redoubt, but moved up in pursuit of the 4th Middlesex who advanced from these trenches at Zero Hour. The parapet of the British front line was being swept by machine-gun fire, and many men were falling without having advanced a single yard. Amongst this chaos Major Stewart Walter Loudoun-Shand was showing his usual leadership qualities. The citation for his Victoria Cross gives a vivid account of what happened:

'When his company attempted to climb over the parapet to attack the enemy's trenches, they were met by very fierce machine-gun fire, which temporarily stopped their progress. Major Loudoun-Shand immediately leapt on the parapet, helped the men over it, and encouraged them in every way until he fell mortally wounded. Even then he insisted on being propped up in the trench, and went on encouraging the non-commissioned officers and men until he died.'[2]

**Major Loudoun-Shand in the action which earned him a posthumous VC.**

Stewart Loudoun-Shand was born in Ceylon on 8th October 1879 into a family that had made a fortune from tea plantations. Educated at Dulwich College, he worked at a bank in the City of London and later served in the Boer War with the Pembroke Yeomanry. By the outbreak of the Great War Loudoun-Shand was back working in Ceylon and returned to England for a commission in the 10th Yorkshire Regiment; serving in France, he was rapidly promoted Major when his battalion suffered heavy officer casualties at the Battle of Loos in September 1915. After Major Loudoun-Shand was killed opposite Fricourt on 1st July his body was brought back by his men for a decent burial in Norfolk Cemetery.

There are good views down

into Fricourt from this vantage point, and further over to the right the high ridge above the village can also be seen. Bois Francais surmounts this position and features in another walk elsewhere in this book. Over to the left La Boisselle and Lochnagar Crater remain clearly visible. Beyond Fricourt is Fricourt Wood, and to the left of that is the site of Crucifix Trench; one of the major objectives of the 21st Division on 1st July. Only a handful of men reached there that day; Fricourt did not fall, and it was several days before all the positions spread out before you were finally captured.

From here **follow the track across the high ground** and down towards Fricourt. You will be crossing over the site of No Man's Land at this point. About half a kilometre further on **a grass path** goes off to the **right** across a field and leading down to a visible military cemetery. **Follow this path**. Before entering the cemetery, pause and look towards Fricourt village.

This cemetery is in No Man's Land where the 10th West Yorkshire Regiment advanced on 1st July. The British lines were due west of the cemetery, and German trenches east towards Fricourt village. The 10th West Yorks left their positions at zero hour, and the first waves succeeded in getting into the German positions around Konig Trench; while on their left a Royal Engineers Tunnelling Company blew several mines on a strongpoint known as The Tambour. The exact number of mines exploded remains a matter of some controversy, and it is thought there were two explosions followed by a third later in the day. However, despite the use of these mines a murderous fire opened on No Man's Land and the following waves were annihilated. Those in Konig Trench were cut off and killed or captured; the small band of survivors crawled back to the British lines after dark. The 10th West Yorks had suffered 710 casualties in the fighting that day; this was the highest casualties in any single battalion for the 1st July 1916. Over fifty percent of this figure were men killed in action; among them the Commanding Officer Lieutenant-Colonel A.Dickson, along with his second in command and adjutant. Indeed, all but one of the officers that accompanied the battalion into action had become casualties.

A follow up attack was made on the afternoon of the 1st July by two companies of the 7th East Yorkshire Regiment, who had previously been held in reserve and occupied the British front line after the 10th West Yorks had advanced. The failure of the 10th in silencing German opposition in Konig Trench, and the general failure of the whole Division both left and right, meant that these men of the 7th East Yorks moved out into No Man's Land facing withering machine-gun fire. Few made it to the German lines, and there were 123 casualties.

## FRICOURT NEW MILITARY CEMETERY

Fricourt New Military Cemetery was made after the capture of Fricourt, when the battlefield was cleared of dead. Indeed some of those involved in the task were the handful of survivors from the 10th West Yorks. Of the 210 burials here, 159 are from the 10th West Yorkshire Regiment and thirty-eight from the 7th East Yorks. There are also two New Zealand soldiers from later fighting. Among the 10th West Yorks men buried here are Lieutenant-Colonel A. Dickson (C-12), with his adjutant Captain J.W. Shann (C-13) buried close by. Dickson's second in command, Major J.L. Knott DSO, was originally buried here but his influential parents arranged for his grave to be moved next to that of his brother at Ypres Reservoir Cemetery in Belgium. This was a rare occurrence, as the War Graves Commission were usually reluctant to move men some distance away from where they were first buried. Another 10th West Yorks soldier in Fricourt New Military Cemetery is Lieutenant Alfred Victor Ratcliffe (C-8); Ratcliffe was a trainee barrister who had published a volume of poetry before the war. He continued to write after joining the West Yorks in 1914, but like many young poets of his generation only became well known after his death. The Ratcliffe family placed a private memorial against their son's headstone, and it is still there today.

**The grave of Lt-Col A Dickson in Fricourt New Military Cemetery**

Graves from the 7th East Yorks make up the other significant proportion of 1st July burials in this cemetery. Among them is that of Pte Albert Edward Barker (B-3); aged only sixteen when he fell on 1st July 1916, he was one of the youngest soldiers to die on that day on any part of the Somme front. From the eastern wall of the cemetery there is a good view across to some scrubland that is the site of the Tambour mine craters. Three craters exist from the 1st July operations, but there were several others from previous mining operations. Today these craters, although well preserved, are on private land and cannot be visited.

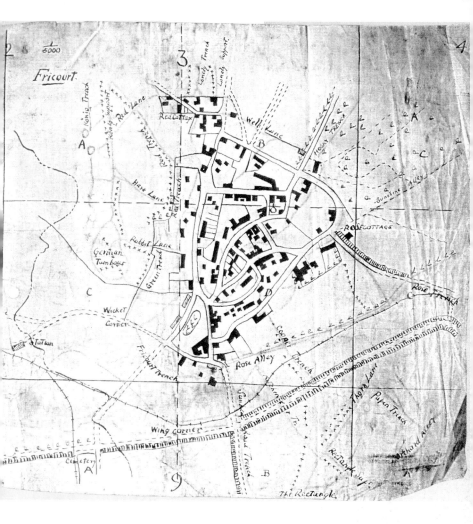

Map issued to officers of the 10th West Yorkshire Regiment showing the German defences around Fricourt.

**Return to the track** via the grass path and **turn right** continuing towards Fricourt. Further on the track meets a better road; follow it into the village – passing an array of barking dogs which inhabit the back gardens here. In Fricourt **turn right** onto the main Contalmaison-Fricourt road (D.147) into the centre of the village. Further on there is a large open area near the war memorial; to the left, up a bank, is a bar among the trees, which is usually open. Otherwise continue past this village square to a minor cross-roads; **go straight on along the D.147**, past a butcher's on your right, and a hundred yards or so further along is another military cemetery.

# FRICOURT (BRAY ROAD) CEMETERY

The ground opposite this cemetery was No Man's Land on 1st July. The British trenches ran at right angles from the roadside wall, and it was here that A Company of the 7th Yorkshires were in the line that morning; forming the 'right of the line' for that battalion. The 7th Yorkshires had been ordered not to take part in the operations against Fricourt, but for some reason A Company's commander, Major R.E.D. Kent, ordered his men forward sometime after zero hour. They came under terrific fire from Fricourt Trench on the outskirts of the village, and most of the company got no further than a few yards from their own front line. Kent himself was severely wounded. The reason why Major Kent took his men over without orders remains a mystery to this day, but no action was ever taken against him. He went on to command the 4th Yorkshires and was killed in bitter fighting on the Chemin des Dames in May 1918[3]. The main body of 7th Yorkshires attacked across ground further north-west from this cemetery on the afternoon of 1st July. Fricourt (Bray Road) Cemetery contains many graves from this battalion – most of them from Major Kent's A Company. Indeed there are eighty-nine graves from the 7th Yorkshires out of a total of 132 burials. The battalion also erected a stone memorial to the fighting of 1st July, which lists all the men from the 7th who died on that day.

Another interesting grave from the later fighting around Fricourt is that of Major Robert George Raper, 8th South Staffordshire Regiment.

**Fricourt village in 1914.**

**Fricourt (Bray Road) Cemetery in 1919.**

This is in fact quite a recent burial, as he originally had a private memorial opposite the current cemetery. Raper was killed in Fricourt Wood on the morning of 2nd July 1916, in a daring attack when a hundred German prisoners were taken. Raper's parents, from Battle in Sussex, purchased the ground on which their son was buried and maintained the site until the mid-1960s, when his remains were moved into this cemetery. He is also commemorated in the village itself with a street named in his honour; Rue Major Raper which leads to the church from the main square.

Leaving the cemetery, **go left** back towards the centre of Fricourt village. At the cross-roads you passed before, now **go left** down a minor road. The German front line just south-west of Fricourt crossed this road a little further along this road and the area was known as Wicket Corner on British maps. The 7th Yorkshires were in the line opposite here, and their attack on the afternoon of 1st July crossed this ground.

Continue along the road; further up there is a branch to the left. Ignore this – it goes to the site of the old Fricourt railway station, now a car breakers yard. Continue on the **right fork** going westwards on the minor road for just over a kilometre – it becomes a cart track further on.

There are good views over to the right, and back towards Fricourt over ground which you have already covered on this walk. This track will eventually bring you out on the minor road that runs from Becordel to Becourt. **Turn right**, and a few hundred yards further up on the right is Norfolk Cemetery and your vehicle.

READING LIST

Sly, J.  'The Mystery of Major Kent' in *Stand To!* The Journal of the Western Front Association Summer 1991 : No 32.

Spicer, L.D.  *Letters From France 1915-18* (Robert York 1979).

# THE POETS' WALK:
## BOIS FRANCAIS AND MAMETZ

STARTING POINT: **Citadel New Military Cemetery, Fricourt-Bray Road (D.147)**
DURATION: **3 hours**
WALK SUMMARY: **This walk takes in the ground around Fricourt and Mametz that was home to Great War poets Siegfried Sassoon and Robert Graves in the 1915/16 period. The walk also covers some of the fighting around Mametz on 1st July 1916, when the poet William Noel Hodgson was killed**.

*Park your vehicle outside Citadel New Military Cemetery, reached by a short track from the Fricourt-Bray road (D.147). Before leaving take time to explore the many interesting graves in the cemetery.*

### CITADEL NEW MILITARY CEMETERY

This cemetery stands near the former site of Citadel Camp, a large bivouac area for units out of the line in Fricourt-Mametz sector which by the end of the Battle of the Somme had become a huge hutted camp. One observer left this description,

'... the camp was situated in a vast plain, devoid of landmarks
and bare and desert-like. They sheltered in contraptions
like chicken hutches, with rabbit wire walls.'[1]

An Advanced Dressing Station (ADS) was also established by the Royal Army Medical Corps. Burials in the military cemetery were started by the French in early 1915, and continued when British troops first came to this area in August of the same year. The first men to be buried were largely from battalions in the 7th Division, which held the Bois Francais sector at that time. One of the battalions in the division was the 1st Royal Welsh Fusiliers (RWF), a veritable 'poets and writers' battalion which has strong associations with the area to be covered in much of this walk. When 1st RWF came to the Bois Francais sector among its junior officers were Siegfried Sassoon, Robert Graves and Bernard Adams; the first two later to become major twentieth century poets. Bernard Adams' fine book *Nothing of Importance* was published

**Bernard Adams**

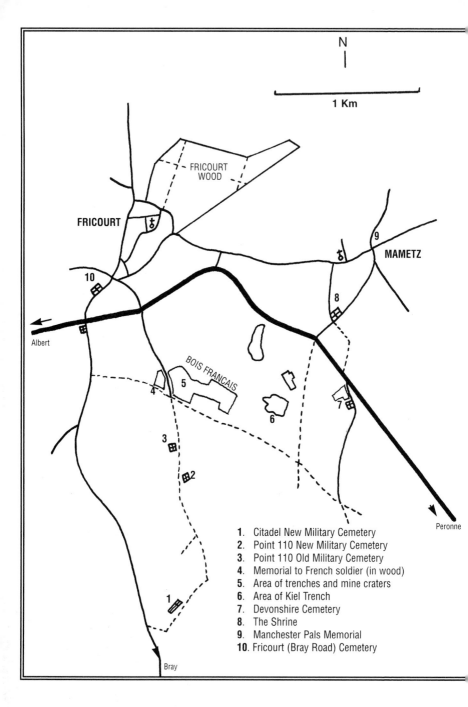

N

1 Km

FRICOURT WOOD

FRICOURT

MAMETZ

9

10

8

Albert

BOIS FRANCAIS

4
5

6

7

3

2

1

Peronne

1. Citadel New Military Cemetery
2. Point 110 New Military Cemetery
3. Point 110 Old Military Cemetery
4. Memorial to French soldier (in wood)
5. Area of trenches and mine craters
6. Area of Kiel Trench
7. Devonshire Cemetery
8. The Shrine
9. Manchester Pals Memorial
10. Fricourt (Bray Road) Cemetery

Bray

after his death in 1917; it recorded his war experiences in the Bois Francais sector until he was wounded and brought back to the ADS at Citadel Camp in June 1916. A quiet, kindly man, he was described by a friend as,'... one of the very best men... best every way, in mind and soul and all his nature.'[2]Adams returned to 1st RWF in January 1917, and after only a few weeks service was seriously wounded leading his men in an attack near Serre. Bernard Adams died of wounds in a Casualty Clearing Station on 27th February 1917 and today is buried in Couin Military Cemetery.

Citadel New Military Cemetery now contains the graves of 379 British soldiers. Among them are many from the pre-Somme Battle period and of particular interest is the grave of Cpl R. O'Brien (III-F-17), 1st RWF, who was brought in from in front of the Bois Francais mine craters by Siegfried Sassoon on 25th May 1916; O'Brien, Sassoon's companion on a raid that night, died of his wounds on the 26th and Sassoon was awarded the Military Cross. Also buried here are many Guards Division officers, who died in the Citadel ADS after being wounded in the fighting around Guillemont and Ginchy in September 1916. Among them was Lieutenant-Colonel Guy Baring (II-A-9), a former Conservative MP who commanded 1st Coldstream Guards, and Captain A.K.S. Cunningham (II-C-3), 2nd Grenadier Guards; Cunningham was the last survivor of the original battalion that had crossed to France in 1914. A high ranking officer, Brigadier-General L.M. Phillpotts CMG DSO (II-A-1), was killed on 8th September 1916, aged forty-six, near Guillemont while serving as the chief artillery officer of the 24th Division; his body was brought back to Citadel Cemetery for burial.

Leaving the cemetery, **turn left** onto the track and follow as it gradually goes uphill. Further along the track bends to the left; **continue towards the wooded area** on the ridge ahead (Bois Francais). After a high point, the track goes downhill to a military cemetery on the right, which is reached by a short grass path across the field.

POINT 110 NEW MILITARY CEMETERY:

This is the first of two original battlefield cemeteries in the area known on British trench maps as Point 110. Point 110 New Military Cemetery contains the graves of sixty-four British burials from February 1916 onwards, when the Old Cemetery became disused. The majority of the graves are men from the 7th Division, and are largely soldiers from the Manchester Pals battalions. Of the 1st RWF burials, three are of particular importance; Second Lieutenant David Thomas, Second Lieutenant David Pritchard and Captain Mervyn Richardson.

**Siegfried Sassoon**

These three died within a day of each other after one officer in the battalion tempted fate by remarking how they had suffered no officer casualties for some months. Siegfried Sassoon and Robert Graves were particularly close to the young David Thomas; both have written about this incident in their memoirs and poetry. Thomas died on 18th March 1916, aged twenty; Pritchard died the next day, along with 'Tracker' Richardson who was mortally wounded by a shell in the front line. Sassoon left this vivid account of David Thomas' funeral in his diaries:

'... tonight I saw his shrouded form laid in the earth with his two companions (young Pritchard was killed this evening also). In the half clouded moonlight the parson stood above the graves, and then everything was dim but the striped flag laid across them. Robert Graves, beside me, with his white whimsical face twisted and grieving. Once we could not hear the solemn words for the noise of a machine-gun along the line; and when all was finished a canister fell a few hundred yards away to burst with a crash.'[3]

Sassoon, in particular, never fully recovered from David Thomas' death (he calls him 'Dick Tiltwood' in *Memoirs of An Infantry Officer*); night after night he went out on raids almost determined to be killed himself. This reckless behaviour earned him the name 'Mad Jack' among the other officers of 1st RWF.

Return via the grass lane and **turn right** onto the track. Further along another military cemetery appears on the left, bordering the track.

The grave of 2/Lt David Thomas ('Dick Tiltwood') Point 110 New Military Cemetery

### POINT 110 OLD MILITARY CEMETERY

This was the original military cemetery at Point 110 and was used from August 1915 until closed in February 1916; possibly because of its closeness to the front line which was among the trees (Bois Francais) on the skyline. The ninety-two British burials are again largely 7th Division men, with some from the 18th (Eastern) Division. This was a

**View towards Bois Francais from Point 110.**

Kitchener's Army division recruited in the south-east and was one of the first such divisions to arrive on the Somme front. There are also a number of graves from men in the Royal Engineer Tunnelling Companies who were involved in the mining operations up at Bois Francais.

A good view up to the ridge on which Bois Francais sits can be obtained from the entrance to this cemetery. Communication trenches ran in the fields here and the cemetery is near the site of Maple Redoubt. This was a large complex and was one of a number of redoubts in the British positions. Well stocked with supplies and equipment, the dugouts here were deep, and often used as battalion headquarters by infantry battalions in the line. It was remembered by Bernard Adams, one of Sassoon's and Graves' fellow officers in 1st RWF:

'... we are in support in a place called Maple Redoubt, on the reverse slope of a big ridge. Good dug-outs, and a view behind, over a big expanse of chalk downs, which is most exhilarating... being on the reverse slope, you can walk about anywhere, and so we can see everything.'[4]

Nothing is visible on the surface to indicate Maple Redoubt ever existed, but the tunnels and dugouts beneath must surely remain.

Come out of the cemetery gate and **turn left**, continuing up the track towards the ridge. At the top the track reaches a large open area and is a form of crossroads. A **diversion to the left** is first taken, following the track downhill past a silage pit on the right to the western edge of

Bois Francais. About a hundred or so yards along the wood, an entrance is seen leading to a memorial commemorating a French soldier.

## MEMORIAL TO FRENCH SOLDIER

This very well kept private memorial is the grave of French soldier H. Tomasin, who died here in early 1915 whilst serving with the 26th Infantry Regiment. The memorial states he was in the 'class of 1900' which indicates Tomasin was in his thirties when he died. After the war the family purchased the ground where their son had fallen, but now it is maintained by Souvenir Francais. Sadly, little else is known of Pte Tomasin. Among the trees, and very close to the grave, trenches and shell holes can be seen. Further exploration of the wood will reveal a network of positions that were once part of the British front line, and beyond them some large mine craters. Private property should be respected, and care taken at all times.

**Return to the track** and follow it back to the crossroads. To the left would take you down into Fricourt, and right to Point 110. Therefore continue straight on **along a new track** with a wired off grass area on the left. Walk about fifty yards along this track and then stop, looking left. The grassed area in this field is one of the few untouched remaining sections of trenches from prior to the Somme fighting. The high banked emplacements are of Second World War vintage; constructed by a French anti-aircraft unit in 1939 to defend the nearby Meaulte airfield. They were used again by the Germans for the same purpose. Beyond and around them, however, are the remains of trenches and shell holes from the Great War. Where the field meets a tree-line are a group of fairly deep mine craters in front of the German position known as Bois Francais Trench. Like those near the French grave, they are evidence of French, British and German mining activities here in the 1915/16 period, when the lines were so close. On 1st July 1916 C Company of the 20th Manchesters (Manchester Pals) successfully attacked across this ground. The area is now private property and in the trees beyond is a 'Ball Trap' (clay pigeon) range where shooting occurs most weekends.

**Continue along the track** and just before reaching another crossroads of tracks, a small copse is visible out in the fields to the left. This copse hides further mine craters and to the left of it was the site of Kiel Trench and Kiel Trench crater. It was here that Siegfried Sassoon won his Military Cross on 25th May 1916; the citation for this award reads:

'For conspicuous gallantry during a raid on the enemy's trenches. He remained for 1½ hours under rifle and bomb fire

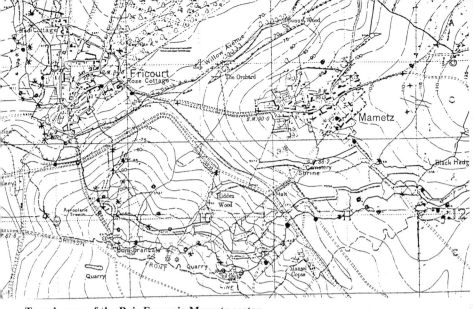

**Trench map of the Bois Francais-Mametz sector.**

collecting and bringing in our wounded. Owing to his courage
and determination all the killed and wounded were brought in.'[5]
Continue on to the crossroads of tracks, and **carry on straight across**
along the now grassier track. As you move along this track there are
splendid views towards Montauban on the left (the church spire is
visible) and Carnoy in the hollow towards the right. About 200 yards
further on is a more obvious **track to the left**, which is metalled. Follow
this down to Mansel Copse and Devonshire Cemetery, reached by a
flight of wood and stone-chipping steps.

## DEVONSHIRE CEMETERY

Devonshire Cemetery stands in a fine location at Mansel Copse, and
contains 163 British burials. All but two of the graves are of men from
the 8th and 9th Battalions of the Devonshire Regiment who fell on 1st
July 1916. The 8th and 9th Devons were Kitchener's Army battalions in
the 7th Division, who had fought at Loos in September 1915. On 1st
July 1916 they attacked from assembly trenches towards German
positions in Danube Trench and beyond. The ground was very difficult,
and once in the open advancing troops could clearly be seen from
Mametz village which boasted a number of machine-gun positions.
Prior to the battle one of the officers in 9th Devonshires, Captain
Duncan Lenox Martin, constructed a model of the Mametz battlefield
and realised that if certain German defences were not silenced by the
preliminary bombardment, he and his men were doomed. His grim
predictions proved true and he fell with many others, enfiladed by

machine-gun fire from The Shrine in Mametz.

**William Noel Hodgson**

Another officer in the 9th Devonshires was Captain William Noel Hodgson. Born in Thornbury, Gloucestershire, he was educated at Durham School and Christ Church College, Oxford. He joined the 9th Devons in September 1914, and won the Military Cross for bravery at the Battle of Loos. Like many of his class and generation, Hodgson was an aspiring poet, but sadly only achieved any celebrity after his death at Mametz on 1st July. A few days before he had completed what became his best known poem, 'Before Action'; he and Martin were obviously very fatalistic, the last stanza of this fine poem clearly hinting at his own death:

> I, that on my familiar hill
> saw with uncomprehending eyes
> A hundred of Thy sunsets spill
> Their fresh and sanguine sacrifice,
> Ere the sun swings his noonday sword
> Must say good-bye to all of this:
> By all delights that I shall miss,
> Help me to die, O Lord.[6]

After the capture of Mametz, the bodies of Hodgson and Martin, along with many of their fellow officers and men, were brought back to a disused trench in Mansel Copse for burial. A wooden board erected on the site recorded the fact that 'The Devonshires Held This Trench, The Devonshires Hold It Still'. When the grave was made permanent by the War Graves Commission in the 1920s, into what is now Devonshire Cemetery, the board had long since disappeared. In 1986 a new memorial bearing this famous legend was unveiled by the Duke of Kent, President of the Commonwealth War Graves Commission and Colonel of the Devon and Dorset Regiment, on the seventieth anniversary of the action. It can be found carved in stone by the entrance to the cemetery.

Return to the metalled track and **turn left**, following it down past a small quarry on the left, until the main Albert-Peronne road (D.938) is reached. **Stop where the track meets road**. You are now on the site of No Man's Land. To the left uphill is the difficult ground over which the 8th and 9th Devons attacked on 1st July. Looking to the right up towards Mametz, the grey vaults of a civilian cemetery are visible on the outskirts of the village. The German front line was half-way between you and the cemetery; the latter was known as The Shrine and the Germans had machine-guns in it. **Turn left** onto the main road and follow it for a short distance until a **cart track** is seen **on the right**. **Follow this** track upwards to Mametz. It comes out near the civilian cemetery, where the track meets a metalled road into the village. Go to the edge of the civilian cemetery and look back. You are now on the site of The Shrine looking downwards to Mansel Copse and the British lines. Further along the ridge the site of the former German reserve positions and Hidden Wood can be seen. It was across this terrain that the 8th and 9th Devonshires suffered such heavy casualties and was where Hodgson and Martin were killed. You are seeing clearly the

**German machine-gunners.**

**The ruins of Mametz July 1916.**

**Fricourt village, 1919.**

potential field of fire of a 1916 German machine-gunner; not a common possibility on the modern Somme battlefield.

Now **follow the metalled road to the right** of the cemetery, which leads you into Mametz. A cross-roads in the village is reached. On the opposite side of the road to the right, next to the village war memorial, a low wall supports a new memorial to the men who fought at Mametz on 1st July 1916. It particularly commemorates the Manchester Pals battalions and was erected by members of the Lancashire and Cheshire Branch of the Western Front Association; one of several memorials this branch has erected on the Somme. From the memorial **go back to the cross-roads** and follow **signs towards Fricourt**, following the main road through Mametz past the church. Rarely open, inside the church is a memorial to the 38th (Welsh) Division. Further along a recently cleared out area for road repair equipment is passed (and often the dumping ground for unexploded shells). **Continue to the outskirts** of the village. The view along a valley towards Fricourt can now be seen. On what becomes the new road, bordered by crash barriers, take the right hand turning signposted for Fricourt. Follow into the village.

Fricourt was a 1st July objective, but eluded capture until the 2nd July when units of the 17th (Northern) Division came into the village and pushed onwards to Fricourt Wood. After the battle Max Plowman described the scene around the village:

'... the country here is a stricken waste... everything needs pointing out, for the general impression is a wilderness without verdue or growth of any kind.'[7]

Entering the village, **follow the road** round to where several streets eventually meet a large square with a tree-lined area. Above it to the right is a bar, which is often open. In the southern corner of the village square **follow the D.147 and signs for Bray**, on the road out of Fricourt. Passing a butcher's on the right, a military cemetery is reached a little further on, on the right.

For details of this cemetery – Fricourt (Bray Road) Cemetery – refer to the Yorkshire Walk on page 124. Returning to the road from the cemetery, **turn right** and continue along to the crossroads where this road meets the main Albert-Peronne road (D.938). **Go straight across** here, continuing to follow signs for Bray on the D.147. This road follows a pretty valley. About one kilometre from the crossroads, the road bends gradually to the left. This is the site of 71 North and 71 South. These were map references on British trench maps, and a place often referred to by Siegfried Sassoon in *Memoirs of An Infantry Officer*. Further deep dugouts, supply dumps and Regimental Aid Posts were established here at various times. Being out of view of the German

# MONTAUBAN 1ST JULY 1916

STARTING POINT: **Carnoy Military Cemetery, Carnoy**
DURATION: **3 hours**
WALK SUMMARY: **This pleasant walk, largely off the beaten track, takes in all the ground around Montauban where men of the 18th (Eastern) and 30th Divisions successfully stormed the German lines on 1st July 1916.**

*Park your vehicle outside Carnoy Military Cemetery; there is ample room to pull right off the road. Before leaving, take time to visit the cemetery.*

## CARNOY MILITARY CEMETERY

Carnoy was a small village, just behind the British front lines, which were taken over from the French in the summer of 1915. It remained very much a quiet sector until the 1916 Battle of the Somme, save the occasional trench raid and artillery shoot. The burials in Carnoy were started in August 1915 by the 2nd King's Own Scottish Borderers and

**Carnoy Military Cemtery, 1919.**

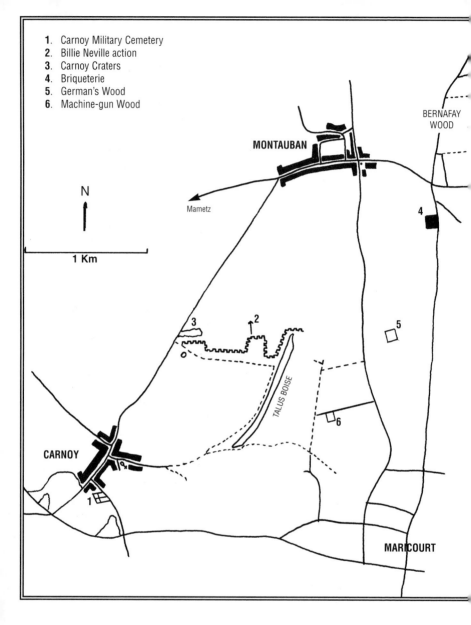

1. Carnoy Military Cemetery
2. Billie Neville action
3. Carnoy Craters
4. Briqueterie
5. German's Wood
6. Machine-gun Wood

BERNAFAY WOOD

MONTAUBAN

Mametz

N

1 Km

4

3

2

TALUS BOISE

5

6

CARNOY

1

MARICOURT

2nd King's Own Yorkshire Light Infantry, battalions from the 5th Division which took over former French trenches from Becourt to the River Somme at this time. The military cemetery stayed in use right through the Battle of the Somme, principally by the many RAMC Field Ambulances which operated in the Carnoy area. The cemetery was closed in March 1917, but a few graves were added later. There are 828 British burials, five New Zealand, two Canadian, one Australian and one South African. The unknown graves are only twenty-nine in number, but there are eighteen Special Memorials to men whose graves were damaged by shell fire.

Perhaps the most visited grave in this cemetery is that of Captain Wilfred Percy Nevill (E-28); it was Nevill's platoon that signalled the start of the Big Push by kicking footballs out across No Man's Land- an extreme example of the war being a 'great game'. The story was taken up by many of the popular newspapers of the day and became world famous. 'Billie' Nevill, as he was known, had joined the 8th East Surrey Regiment in 1915, but was actually commissioned into the East Yorkshire Regiment; indeed his headstone bears that regiment's cap badge. Elsewhere the cemetery reflects the high price paid in senior officers during the Somme fighting. Lieutenant-Colonel H.L. Budge (E-9), aged thirty-eight and a veteran of the Boer War, was killed commanding the 12th Royal Scots near Longueval on 13th July 1916. Lieutenant-Colonel R.J.W. Carden (S-22), aged forty, was a regular army 17th Lancers officer who died commanding the 16th Royal Welch Fusiliers at Mametz Wood on 10th July 1916. Buried next to each other are: Lieutenant-Colonel J.S.M. Lenox-Conyngham (R-33) of the 6th Connaught Rangers, who fell at Ginchy on 3rd September 1916, aged fifty-four, and Lieutenant-Colonel F.E.P. Curzon (R-34), aged fifty-seven, who died six days later on 9th September leading the 6th Royal Irish Regiment- also at Ginchy.

Leaving the cemetery by the main gate, **turn left** onto the road and follow it to a cross-roads in the village. At the **cross-roads turn right** onto the D.213E for Montauban, but after a few hundred yards, **turn right again** at the village war memorial. Follow this minor road, past

**Carnoy village 1915: the marie (left) and the church.**

**View across Carnoy towards Montauban, 1915.**

the Mairie on the left and the church ahead. At the church the road forks; **take the left fork** into Rue de la Plaine and follow it downhill out of the village. On the outskirts a wood, Talus Boise, will be visible ahead to the left – the road eventually becomes a track. This track was a main route up to the front line around Talus Boise– a long narrow wood running north-east into the British lines. By 1916 the wood was full of dugouts, machine-gun and trench mortar emplacements. A light railway also ran along this track and was used to evacuate wounded on 1st July 1916. Many battalions were held in support here before going up to the front line opposite Montauban; the ground is out of view of the former German positions, which are in the far distance to your left.

Just beyond where the metalled road ends there is a junction of tracks; ignore the track which goes off to the left and take the **right hand** one. Further along is another junction of tracks; again ignore the other tracks and **continue straight on**. The track you are on eventually runs along the western edge of Talus Boise. The further you go, the more Montauban becomes visible on the skyline – especially the distinctive bulbous church spire. Continue along the edge of Talus Boise until the track turns sharply to the left. **Stop**. From here – and further along this new track – there are good views ahead to Montauban, and the ground over which men of the 18th (Eastern) Division advanced on 1st July. The 18th Division was a Kitchener's

Army formation raised in August and September 1914 largely from battalions of Home Counties regiments. The division had been on the Somme since the summer of 1915, but this was their first major action. The front line trenches of 55 Brigade were just to the north of the track on rising ground to the left, and men of the 7th Queen's, 7th Buffs, 7th Royal West Kents and 8th East Surreys all advanced here on 1st July. Major D.F. Grant, commanding A Battery of 84th Brigade Royal Field Artillery, and supporting the attack of 55th Brigade, observed the attack from an Observation Post on the Peronne road near Carnoy,

> '... the morning of 1st July was misty... and it was feared [we] would not see the actual attack. However, a few minutes before 7.30am, zero time, the mist thinned, and... we were able to see the 7th Queen's, whom we were covering, and the 8th East Surreys on their right, forming up in front of their trenches. The long line of men forming up in front of our front line was a wonderful sight, and only eclipsed as one saw them go across No Man's Land. The 8th East Surreys led off with a football, which incident is now famous in history.'[1]

The main assault was on Breslau Trench, which was duly reached and the men of 55th Brigade began bombing their way up communication trenches towards Montauban. Captain Billie Nevill had indeed led his platoon forward with footballs, but he had fallen near the German trenches to the left of Talus Boise.

**Follow this track** going off to the left from Talus Boise; it rises up slightly and there are good views to the right towards Montauban

**The trench system before Montauban.**

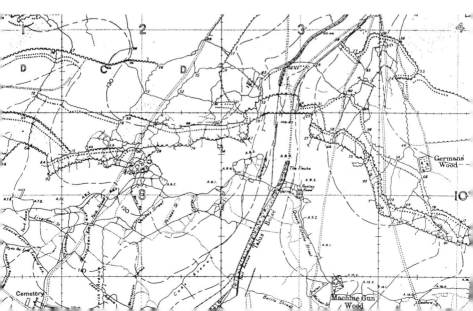

**The Carnoy Craters, 2 July, 1916.**

village. On clear days the trees of Bernafay Wood are visible to the right of Montauban. This track also skirts the former front line of 1st July. Stay on the track until it joins a metalled road; the D.213E Carnoy-Montauban. **Turn right onto the road**. A few yards on the right is an area of rough ground and scrub. **Stop**. The area of scrub and trees marks an area that was once littered with mine craters which divided the British and German trenches opposite Montauban. Although some degree of filling in has taken place in recent years, several old craters still exist, but continue to be used as rubbish tips. Most of these craters dated from mining activity prior to the Somme battle, but a few mines were exploded near here on 1st July. The most famous was at Casino Point, located some distance to the left of the Carnoy-Montauban road, which was blown late on 1st July causing casualties and confusion among the advancing men of 18th Division. Sadly, it too has been filled in.

Another well known incident took place near here on 1st July. Major D.F. Grant of 84th Brigade RFA related his version of events:

'... it was on the Divisional front, and on the edge of the 'lane' allotted to A/84, that a German machine-gunner was found chained to his M.G. in his concrete covered emplacement – to

144

prevent him running away. However, this fellow was a stout and brave soldier, for he would not surrender, and had to be shot, having caused considerable casualties to our infantry long after the main attack had passed beyond him.'[2]

From the Carnoy craters, follow the main road to Montauban. There are good views towards the village as you go further up. On the outskirts of Montauban, near a steel fence post on the left, turn round and look back over the ground you have just walked. From here you have a superb view over the Montauban battlefield, from the German perspective. From left to right the following are visible: Machine Gun Wood, Maricourt, Talus Boise and Carnoy. **Return to the the road**, and follow it into the village; it soon joins the D.64 Mametz-Montauban road. At this junction **turn right** into Montauban itself, and stay on the road as it passes the church and Mairie.

Montauban was a large village several hundred yards behind the German lines north of Carnoy and Talus Boise. It was well defended, and even by 1st July was still in fairly good condition. The strong defence line of Montauban Alley trench ran to the north of the village, and to the south it was flanked by Southern Trench that ringed this part of Montauban from British attacks. On 1st July 1916 men of the 18th Division had fought effectively beyond Talus Boise and made their way up through the German communication trenches, the 7th Royal West Kents and 7th Buffs reaching the western edge of the village by the close of fighting that day. The village itself was captured by units of the 30th Division, attacking alongside 18th Division and to the right of Talus Boise. The 16th and 17th Manchesters (Manchester City Pals)

**Amongst the ruins of Montauban all that remains is a statue of the Virgin Mary.**

**The main street of Montauban, 1914.**

assaulted Southern Trench and fought their way through the village to Montauban Alley, which they occupied and then fought off many counter-attacks. Overall the attack on Montauban was very much a success, with minimal casualties compared to other areas along the 1st July front. This is largely attributed to the fact there was a much greater concentration of heavy guns involved in the preliminary bombardment here. Loaned by the French, they effectively smashed the deep German strong points and there was little problem with uncut wire.

**Continuing through Montauban** a junction just before the eastern outskirts of the village is reached. Signposts over to the left indicate Bazentin and green CWGC signs show directions for Quarry Cemetery. On the right, set on a small green, is a recent memorial which commemorates the part played by the Pals battalions who attacked Montauban on 1st July. In particular it remembers the Liverpool and Manchester City Pals battalions; between them they suffered 1,500 casualties in the fighting here. Unveiled in 1994, this memorial was funded and raised by members of the Liverpool Branch of the Western Front Association. From here **follow the minor road** that runs to the **right of the memorial**, taking you south out of Montauban. **Continue**

**along this road**; it soon becomes sunken and brings you out to a wide plain. There are good views to the left towards Bernafay Wood and some scrubland. This latter area on the far left is the site of the Montauban brickworks, the Briqueterie, which was assaulted and captured by men of the 20th King's Liverpool Regiment (Liverpool Pals) on 1st July. The Briqueterie was quite an extensive complex with deep dugouts; its tall chimney doubled as an Observation Post and was still standing – although badly damaged – when the Somme battle began.

**Continue along the road** as it climbs uphill out of this small valley to the high ground beyond. Over the rise, there are again good views across the Montauban battlefield. From here the attack area of the 30th Division is clearly visible. This division was another Kitchener's Army formation composed largely of Pals battalions from Liverpool and Manchester. This part of the line also marked the junction of the British and French armies on the Somme front. The French 39th Division attacked to the immediate right of the 30th Division on 1st July; the 17th King's Liverpools were the right of the line and attacked alongside their French comrades. Going across the skyline ahead of you, German's Wood is seen on the left, with Maricourt visible in the distance, Machine Gun Wood alone in the fields and then the dark mass of Talus Boise on the right. Pte Harry Redhead, 20th King's Liverpools (4th Liverpool Pals), was one of the Pals who fought here on 1st July and later recalled his experiences:

> '... on July 1st I went over as a Stokes mortar shell carrier. I carried six, each weighing 11lbs so the extra 66lbs, in addition to my other goods – gun, ammunition and two Mills bombs – was a bit much. I reached the captured Jerry trench rather exhausted.'[3]

**Continue along the road**, eventually passing German's Wood on the left. Two hundred yards further on a cart track appears **on the right**. **Follow this** towards Talus Boise. There are good views from here towards Maricourt – you are in fact standing just in front of the German line known as Alt Trench which was captured by Harry Redhead's 20th King's Liverpools on 1st July. Carry on along the

**Harry Redhead
20th King's Liverpool
Regiment**

track towards Talus Boise; a T-junction of tracks is soon reached. Go left in the direction of Maricourt and parallel with Talus Boise itself. Stay on this track, passing Machine Gun Wood in a field on the left; as it goes downhill a track appears **on the right**. **Follow this** winding, partly sunken track towards Talus Boise. **Stay on this track** as it, too, goes downhill to the bottom of Talus Boise. It then continues along the edge of the wood and beyond it meets up with the original track you took out of Carnoy. **Rejoin this track and follow it** back into Carnoy village. The track soon rejoins the metalled Rue de la Plaine, which itself leads to the church. At the church follow the road right and down past the war memorial to meet the D.213E Montauban road. **Go left** here towards the outskirts of Carnoy – a road soon appears on the left; follow it back to Carnoy Military Cemetery and your vehicle.

## READING LIST

Maddocks, G.   *Liverpool Pals* (Pen & Sword 1991)
Stedman, M.   *Manchester Pals* (Pen & Sword 1994)

# BEHIND THE LINES WALK

STARTING POINT: **Church, Auchonvillers**
DURATION: **3½ hours**
WALK SUMMARY: **This walk covers some of the back areas around Auchonvillers, Mailly-Maillet and Englebelmer. Many of these villages survived the war with little damage and original buildings can be seen. Cemeteries associated with Field Ambulances and Advanced Dressing Stations are also visited.**

*Park your vehicle in front of the church in Auchonvillers. The church is in a minor road that becomes a cul-de-sac, and there is no problem with parking here.*

Auchonvillers was a prosperous village of 450 inhabitants before the Great War, known locally for its orchards and walnut trees. French troops arrived in the village in September 1914 and established a trench system east of the village towards the German positions around Beaumont-Hamel. Many of the houses and cellars in the village were used by the French as billets, stores and for medical purposes. British troops first came to Auchonvillers in July 1915, when the 4th Division arrived after being involved in heavy fighting during the Second Battle of Ypres. This was a 'cushy' sector then, where the French and Germans had operated a 'live and let live' system. The British set about improving the defences in the village and on the Mailly-Maillet road established a proper Advanced Dressing Station (ADS). By the 1916 Battle of the Somme much of the village was in ruins and only the cellars remained. It was commonly known to most British soldiers as 'Ocean Villas'. Poet Edmund Blunden was based in

**Auchonvillers church, 1914.**

149

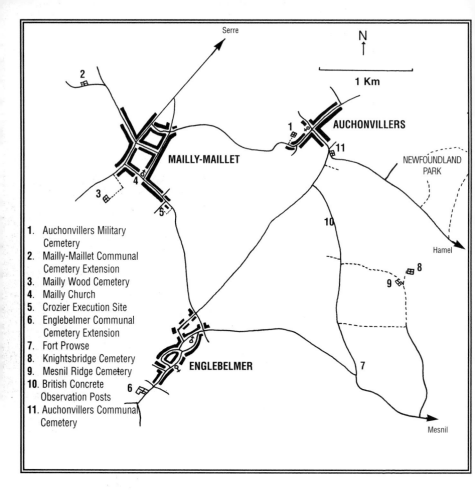

1. Auchonvillers Military Cemetery
2. Mailly-Maillet Communal Cemetery Extension
3. Mailly Wood Cemetery
4. Mailly Church
5. Crozier Execution Site
6. Englebelmer Communal Cemetery Extension
7. Fort Prowse
8. Knightsbridge Cemetery
9. Mesnil Ridge Cemetery
10. British Concrete Observation Posts
11. Auchonvillers Communal Cemetery

Auchonvillers during September 1916, when he was field works officer to the 11th Royal Sussex Regiment (1st South Downs), and left this description:

'The heart of the village is masked with its hedges and orchards from almost all ground observation. That heart nevertheless bleeds. The old homes are razed to the ground, all but one or two, which play involuntary tricks upon probability, balancing themselves like mad acrobats... the church maintains a kind of conceptional shape, and has a cliff-like beauty in the sunlight.'[1]

Leaving the church make for the **cross-roads** in the centre of the village and **turn right** on the D.73 following road-signs for Mailly-Maillet. The road is straight at first then winds to the right and on the outskirts

150

of the village a green CWGC sign for Auchonvillers Military Cemetery is visible on the right. **Follow the grass path** up through the trees to the cemetery.

## AUCHONVILLERS MILITARY CEMETERY

French medical units began this cemetery in June 1915, and it was taken over by the British a month later when 12th Field Ambulance RAMC arrived in Auchonvillers and established an ADS in the farm complex known as Red Barn; the modern replacement of the farm can be seen from the cemetery. The first graves, now in Plot I, were from units of the 4th Division of which 12th Field Ambulance was a part. The 36th (Ulster) Division, on their first tour of the

**The bell of Auchonvillers Church used as a gas alarm, as mentioned by Edmund Blunden in** *Undertones of War.*

trenches in France, continued with burials in the same plot. As the war progressed, and during the Somme battle, the graves were laid out in rows, largely in chronological order. All but fifteen graves are original; these were brought in from the local area and re-buried in Plot II, Row M. They were largely men from the New Zealand Division who fell in 1918. Today Auchonvillers Military Cemetery has 496 British burials, twenty-four New Zealand and eight Newfoundland. Among the early graves is a mass plot at II-A-14 commemorating a number of men in 252nd Tunnelling Company Royal Engineers who died in mining operations below the Redan and Hawthorn Ridges. Other tunnellers from 252nd Tunnelling Company are found elsewhere in the cemetery. There are many graves from the 1st July fighting on Hawthorn Ridge; in particular men from the 1st Royal Dublin Fusiliers and 16th Middlesex Regiment (Public Schools Battalion). One of these was Pte Richard Dale Lovett (II-E-5) who died of wounds in the ADS on 1st July 1916, aged forty-six. The register records '... he left his coffee estate in India and returned to serve in the war'.

**Aerial view of Auchonvillers looking west towards Mailly-Maillet, mid-1916.**

Return to the main road via the grass path and **turn right** onto the road, back in the direction of Mailly-Maillet. Some small buildings further along on the left are the remains of the old railway station, and a sunken road on the right is the route of the old track; in 1916 this was utilised and a line ran to Mailly and beyond. As you walk along this

**Auchonvillers Military Cemetery, 1919.**

route look around in the fields to left and right; this area in 1915/16 was where the Royal Field Artillery had many gun positions. For the preliminary bombardment prior to 1st July, field guns were almost wheel to wheel here firing on the German trenches on Redan and Hawthorn Ridges. Continue along the road into Mailly-Maillet village. Stop at the road junction on the outskirts, **turn left** at the Stop sign and turn **immediate right** at the road which has the '15 T' sign; Rue Elisa Brassart. Pass houses and farm buildings, and at the end **turn left** onto the main D.919, Rue Leon Brevival. This road takes you past the Post Office on the right to a cross-roads in the village. **Turn right** here into Rue Leleu following signs for the D.129 to Colincamps. The road goes downhill, then where it forks at a calvary, follow the green CWGC signs to the left to Mailly-Maillet Communal Cemetery Extension.

**Mailly-Maillet Communal Cemetery early 1920s.** *Julian Sykes*

## MAILLY-MAILLET COMMUNAL CEMETERY EXTENSION

This cemetery was started next to a local civilian cemetery by French troops after the fighting around Serre in 1915. British medical units set up several Field Ambulances in Mailly-Maillet from August 1915 onwards, and began to use the cemetery from that date for men who

153

died of wounds. It was then used until December 1916 and again from March to July 1918. Occasionally the graves of men who had died in the front line trenches were brought back for burial. Today the French burials have been removed, but the Communal Cemetery Extension contains the graves of 122 British soldiers, three New Zealand and one Newfoundlander. Many graves are from units which were serving in the Redan-Hawthorn Ridge sectors. One of the men involved in the laying of the Hawthorn mine is buried here; Spr G.W. Osborne (C-13), 252nd Tunnelling Company Royal Engineers, who died of wounds on 25th January 1916. A Newfoundland officer who survived his battalion's annihilation on 1st July 1916, only to be killed by shell-fire in billets at Colincamps a week later, was Lieutenant Owen Steele (D-10). Aged twenty-nine, he was a native Newfoundlander. A rare private memorial can also be seen on the grave of Pte A. Stevenson (B-19) of 1/7th Argyll & Sutherland Highlanders. He died of wounds received in an early tour of the Somme trenches on 16th September 1915. Good views of the village can also be obtained from the cemetery gate. Looking to the left, there were many gun positions around the old quarries and beyond the ridge is Serre and Redan Ridge. To the right Mailly Woods are clearly visible; the woods were the home to many soldiers out of the line with vast hutted camps in evidence by 1916.

**Return** to Mailly-Maillet the same way, back up the hill into the village. At the **cross-roads turn right** into the main street. There is a fine and well-kept war memorial on the left, which is worth a look. Continue along the main street, with its many original buildings often showing signs of shell and shrapnel damage from the Great War. At a junction further along, continue straight on following the D.919 in the direction of Acheux. A high wall now appears on the left, and where this ends on the outskirts of the village a green CWGC sign is visible for Mailly Wood Cemetery. **Follow the cart track** which leads from the main road up and right to the cemetery.

MAILLY WOOD CEMETERY

The original of this cemetery was established just before the Battle of the Somme by the burial of thirteen men of the 2nd Seaforth Highlanders (4th Division) who died on 25th June 1916. These were among over fifty casualties when the bivouacs of this battalion were shelled; most were killed or injured by the explosion of just one shell. Burials continued through the Somme battle, with the majority of graves being men who died of wounds received in the Redan-Hawthorn Ridge sectors. Further burials were again made in April-August 1918, particularly by units in the 12th (Eastern) Division which did much to

**Mailly Wood Cemetery.**

stop the German advance in this area. These graves are now in Plot II.
After the war a number of small cemeteries existed in Mailly-Maillet,
often containing burials from the many Field Ambulances which were
established in the village. Several of these were closed and the graves
moved into Mailly Wood, and today the cemetery contains the graves of
624 British soldiers, twenty-seven New Zealand and three South
Africans.

Of the 1916 burials there are many officers and men from the
successful attack of 51st (Highland) Division on Beaumont-Hamel on
13th November. Indeed, these graves and the original Seaforth burials
give the cemetery very much a Scottish feel. Also of interest is the
grave of Captain Herbert Geoffrey Lush-Wilson (Sp Mem Q-2). A
regular army officer in the Royal Horse Artillery, Lush-Wilson was the
son of His Honour Sir Herbert Lush-Wilson KC. Before the war he had
distinguished himself as a good horseman and won prizes in the
Military Tournament for fencing. Serving in Y Battery, he fought at
Gallipoli with the 29th Division and he and his battery came to France
with that division in April 1916. He was awarded the Chevalier of the
Legion of Honour, and was killed near Mailly by counter-battery fire on
21st July 1916. A Victoria Cross winner from 1918 can also be found
here; Sergeant Harold John Colley VC MM (II-Q-4) was posthumously
awarded the supreme medal for gallantry whilst serving with the 10th
Lancashire Fusiliers at Martinpuich on 25th August 1918- a long way

155

**Mailly-Maillet church, 1914. The ornate facade was protected by sandbags during the war.** *Julian Sykes*

from Mailly-Maillet, which suggests the grave was brought into the cemetery after the war.

Return to the main Mailly-Acheux road via the cart track, and **turn right** on the road back into the village. At the junction, **turn right** on the D.129 for Englebelmer and follow this street to the church. Again this street has many old buildings in it, most of which show some signs of shell-damage from the Great War. The church is worth a visit; although it is rarely open the sixteenth century facade alone is worthy of closer inspection. Its intricate detail was largely preserved by a quick thinking officer who ordered the front of the church to be sandbagged up in 1916. The spire was destroyed by shell-fire and replaced, but the main body of the church is original. In the winter of 1916/17 the fighting had moved on to beyond Beaumont-Hamel and Mailly-Maillet was less shelled; some of the sandbags must have been moved or come away as several British soldiers left their mark in the stone around the main church doors. Some are less visible than others, but those most obvious are:

D. HUTT [Pnr Dick Hutt Royal Engineers]
T.G. MUSGROVE [Pte Thomas G. Musgrove Army Service Corps]
G. STEER [Pte George H. Steer Army Service Corps]

**P .BLACKLEDGE** [Pte Percy Blackledge Army Service Corps]

Blackledge's inscription also bears the legend "1914-1916, MT ASC" which indicates he had served in a Motor Transport company. Another piece of graffiti shows just the initials of a soldier in the 5/6th Royal Scots – an infantry battalion of the 32nd Division which served in the Beaumont-Hamel sector in late 1916 and was billeted in Mailly-Maillet at that time.

From the church **continue on the D.129 for Englebelmer**. The road slopes downhill as it goes out of Mailly-Maillet and the wall of some chateau grounds are visible on the right. It was behind these walls that one of several executions were carried out in Mailly-Maillet. On this occasion it was Pte James Crozier of the 9th Royal Irish Rifles, who was Shot at Dawn for desertion on 27th February 1916, aged eighteen. Crozier had joined under age in 1914, and his namesake, Lieutenant-Colonel F.P. Crozier, commanding 9th Royal Irish Rifles, had promised James Crozier's mother he would keep an eye on her son. In the end it was the Colonel's testimony that largely secured the fate of young Crozier. On the morning of the execution 9th Royal Irish Rifles were lined up in the road you are standing in, and although they could not see the execution, they could hear it. Commonwealth War Graves Commission records indicate that James Crozier was buried in the grounds of the chateau, but his grave was moved to Sucrerie Cemetery, near Colincamps (see Pals Walk).

**Lt-Col F P Crozier**

**Continue** along the road to Englebelmer. In 1916 the fields to the left and right were the site of further gun positions and bivouacs for troops out of the line around Beaumont-Hamel and Hawthorn Ridge. The outskirts of Englebelmer are soon reached; this was once a separate hamlet known as Vitermont and is still marked thus on modern maps, but today it is indistinguishable from the rest of Englebelmer. At a cross-roads, with Auchonvillers signposted to the left, **take the Rue Neuve to the right** and follow a T-junction. At the **junction turn left**, past the school playground and at the end **turn right** into the main street that runs through Englebelmer. **Follow the road** as it turns left, then right and past a new church on the left. **Continue** through the village for about 200 yards and then **turn right** at a junction following signs for Stade Municipal; the cemetery gates are visible on the right, opposite a football field. Go through the cemetery gates, and graves are seen to the left and right.

This is ENGLEBELMER COMMUNAL CEMETERY in which fifty-one British soldiers and one New Zealander are buried. It was the original cemetery in the village – Englebelmer being used for billeting battalions returning from the trenches in the Beaumont-Hamel sector. Poet Edmund Blunden was here with the 11th Royal Sussex Regiment and called Englebelmer '... a sweet village scarcely yet spoiled'. However, even after a few days in the village during September 1916 heavy shells fell cratering pretty apple orchards and demolishing old houses, throwing the debris into the street. Medical units also occupied the village and a Casualty Clearing Station was established during the Battle of the Somme. Among the British graves in the Communal Cemetery, in II-B is a row of five men from the 2nd York and Lancaster Regiment, all of whom died on 13th August 1916 while the battalion was holding the line at Hamel. Most of the other graves are from the July-August 1916 period, with a few 1918 burials. Continue past the French civilian graves to the gate of the Communal Cemetery Extension.

ENGLEBELMER COMMUNAL CEMETERY EXTENSION
This cemetery was used during the latter part of the 1916 Somme fighting. There are 120 British and twenty-eight New Zealand graves, along with two Special Memorials. The majority of the burials are men who died in the Ancre fighting, among them several of Edmund Blunden's Royal Sussex Regiment (Sp Mem by the gate). Also of interest is the grave of RSM G.B. Wall of 2nd KOYLI who died of wounds on 10th February 1917, aged thirty-seven; the inscription on his headstone reads 'He died fighting'. Row A, at the back of the cemetery, contains the graves of eight men of the Royal Naval Division Engineers who died on 20th October 1916; this unit was formed from the Deal Division, Royal Marines. In the same row is the rare appearance of some cavalry headstones; three men of the 2nd Life Guards who died in Englebelmer on 28th December 1916.

Leaving the cemetery by the same way you came in, **return** to the road and then **to the junction** on the outskirts of Englebelmer. Go back through the village, past the modern church and where the road goes left, fork right down Rue d'En Bas. This takes you past the back of the old, original church. Edmund Blunden visited it in September 1916 and recounts that and many other adventures in Englebelmer in *Undertones of War*. The church bears a few scars from the war, but is rarely open. Continue on to where the road behind the church reaches a T-junction; **turn right**, then **right again in the fork of a road** following signs for the C.5 to Mesnil. Along this route is an area of dead ground used by

Officers of the Northamptonshire Regiment photographed among the ruins of Englebelmer, summer 1916.

the artillery and for bivouacing troops in 1916. Follow this pleasant road for **two kilometres** until it joins the Auchonvillers-Mesnil road; **turn in the direction of Auchonvillers**. You are now on high ground, with commanding views. Here you have a wide view across the Ancre Valley. From left to right: Newfoundland Park, Ancre Heights, Schwaben Redoubt, Thiepval village, Thiepval Memorial, Aveluy Wood and just beyond in the distance on a clear day the spire of the Basilica and tower of the town hall in Albert are visible.

**Continue** along the road in the direction of Auchonvillers; about 150 yards further on there is a small valley to the right. This was the area of Fort Prowse, a reserve defensive position named after Bertie Prowse, 1st Somerset Light Infantry, who as a Brigadier-General was fatally wounded at Serre on 1st July 1916 (see Pals Walk). Prowse also has a cemetery named after him in the Ypres Salient, and his grave can be found in Louvencourt Cemetery. Among the clump of trees in the middle of this valley are the remains of a concrete dugout, which formed the central part of Fort Prowse. At some time it was struck by a large shell, and is partially demolished. **Continue** for about another 150 yards along the main road and a **cart track** is visible on the right. **Take this track** downhill, past a large wired-off area of grazing land until it meets another track at the bottom. You are now in a small valley that runs from Mesnil up to Auchonvillers. In 1916 there were many gun sites here, and it was the route of a light railway which once ran from Albert to Doullens. **Go left on this new track**, past a quarry and follow to a bend in the track where there are two military cemeteries. **Take a grass path** across the field to Knightsbridge Cemetery.

## KNIGHTSBRIDGE CEMETERY

Knightsbridge was an area some distance behind the British lines between Auchonvillers and Hamel, where a light railway ran to Mesnil and an Advanced Dressing Station was established. It was part of the main evacuation route for men wounded in the Hamel area down to the Casualty Clearing Station in Mesnil. The cemetery was begun on 1st July 1916, as wounded men from the 29th Division passed through the ADS; many to die of their wounds. Bodies of the dead which had also clogged the reserve trenches in what is now the Newfoundland Park were also brought back for burial, among them several from the Newfoundland Regiment. The cemetery was used all through the Ancre Heights fighting, and the majority of the graves are men from the 39th Division who fell at Hamel on 3rd September, and the Royal Naval Division from the Beaucourt action of 13th November. After the war Knightsbridge was enlarged by the addition of 112 graves from all over the Somme battlefield. Today, the cemetery commemorates 425 men from British units, thirty-nine from Newfoundland, eighteen New Zealand, one Australian and sixty-five unknown. Among the burials are several interesting individuals: Second Lieutenant W.D. Ayre (B-10) of the Newfoundland Regiment was one of five members of a large Newfoundland to die on 1st July 1916. Captain Francis Ashmead-Bartlett (B-33) is buried in a row of 4th Bedfordshire Regiment officer graves, all of whom died on 13th November 1916. He was the son of a famous journalist who had published a damning book about the conduct of the Gallipoli campaign.

**Return** via the grass path to the main track, cross it via another path and follow the cut-grass to the next military cemetery.

## MESNIL RIDGE CEMETERY

This cemetery predates Knightsbridge and was begun by units of the 4th Division in 1915 when they arrived in the Auchonvillers sector; the first burials were from the 1st Rifle Brigade and are now in Row K. The 36th (Ulster) Division then took over the cemetery, and men who died in the division's first few tours of the line were buried at Mesnil Ridge. The cemetery remained in use until 1st July, when Knightsbridge was opened, although a few graves were added after that date. By the close of the war there were ninety-four British soldiers and one Newfoundlander laid to rest here. Among the graves in Row B are those of Pte Charles Stuart and Pte George Brown of the 11th East Yorkshire Regiment who were killed on 29th March 1916 (B-12/13). Stuart and Brown were the first men to die in France from a brigade of Pals battalions all recruited in Hull. Two graves away is the first man to die from a sister battalion – 13th East Yorkshires – Pte Charles Watts (B-11); Stuart and Watts both lived in the same street in Hull. The cemetery register also records that Pte James Anderson of the 9th Inniskilling Fusiliers (I-11) died on 5th May 1916, '... killed in enemy air raid'.

Leave via the cemetery gate and **turn left**, following a track that was the line of the old railway. This goes gradually uphill until it meets the main D.174. **Turn right** onto the main road and follow towards Auchonvillers, which is visible on the skyline ahead. As the road turns to the left, two British concrete observation posts are visible in the fields just by the road on the left. These were constructed prior to 1st July to enable staff officers and forward observation officers to observe the German positions on Hawthorn Ridge across to the Thiepval ridge. The first one looks towards Thiepval, the second to Hawthorn Ridge and the Newfoundland Park. Both are well made, and one has indents in the concrete surround where sandbags once covered it. Although they are on private ground, access to them is gained with few problems. **Continue** along the road until it meets another, which runs from Englebelmer to Auchonvillers. **Turn right** for Auchonvillers. On the outskirts of the village the road meets a complex junction and veers to the left. Opposite, across an expanse of grass, are the green gates of the local civilian cemetery. Walk across and **go in the gate**, **turning left** and making for the northern edge of the cemetery where British headstones can be seen.

This is AUCHONVILLERS COMMUNAL CEMETERY. Buried here are fifteen British soldiers, thirteen of whom served with the 1st Border Regiment and died on 6th April 1916, when a large shell pitched into Tipperary Avenue communication trench whilst the 1st Borders were moving up to the front line. Of the thirteen, most of them served at Gallipoli and many were regular soldiers, often of some service. Among them is CSM Albert Cormack who died aged thirty-seven, and had over twenty years in the army; having been awarded the Long Service and Good Conduct Medal. The other two graves are of men who died in 1915 and 1918; they were originally buried elsewhere in the cemetery, but their graves were moved in with the others after the Second World War. A large number of French graves from the 293rd Infantry Regiment were once also in this cemetery; they were moved to an unknown location after the Great War. The CWGC headstones here are unusual – they are of red Corsehill stone, which is rarely seen on the Somme.

Go **back to the road** and junction, and return to the centre of Auchonvillers via Rue Delattre, and just further on the church and your vehicle is reached.

## READING LIST

Blunden, E.        *Undertones of War* (Cobden-Sanderson 1928)
Crozier, F.P.       *A Brass Hat in No Man's Land* (Cape 1930)
Putkowski, J. &   *Shot At Dawn* (Leo Cooper 1989)
Sykes, J.

# THE DAWN ATTACK:
# LONGUEVAL 14TH JULY 1916

STARTING POINT: **Quarry Cemetery, Montauban**
DURATION: **3 hours**
WALK SUMMARY: **This walk covers the area over which the 9th (Scottish) Division advanced on Longueval on the morning of 14th July and also ground where the 3rd Division fought near Bazentin-le-Grand the same morning. A visit to Delville Wood is included, where the South African Brigade fought.**

*Park your vehicle outside Quarry Cemetery which is just east of the Montauban to Bazentin-le-Grand road. There are very good parking facilities here, on good ground off the road. Before embarking on the walk take time to see the graves here in this pretty and secluded cemetery.*

## QUARRY CEMETERY, MONTAUBAN

This cemetery is located, as its name suggests, in the site of an old quarry which was used by RAMC Field Ambulances from July 1916 onwards. The first burials were from the fighting of 14th July, and these original ones can be found in Plots V and VI. At the close of the war there were 152 graves in the cemetery and it was then enlarged by the concentration of burial sites from the surrounding area. There are now 648 British graves, thirty-six New Zealand, twenty-five Australian, six South African and twenty-eight Special Memorials. Graves from the Dawn Attack of 14th July are well represented, among them Captain and Adjutant A.G. Hutcheson MC (II-C-2) who was killed attacking Longueval windmill, aged twenty-one. A number of Royal Field Artillery burials represent the changing nature of this ground after the 14th July advance- the valley in which the cemetery stands was used for battery positions during the attacks on High Wood and Longueval fighting. Other interesting graves include a sixteen year old Air Mechanic of 3rd Squadron Royal Flying Corps; R.A. Hobbs (V-G-19) who died near here on 29th August 1916. It is possible he was on signalling duties attached to the RFA. An early tank crew grave can be found at III-H-9; Pte F. Horrock served with the Heavy Branch Machine Gun Corps, although his headstone carries their later badge – the Tank Corps. He is recorded as having died on 25th September 1916; ten days after tanks were used for the first time.

Leaving the cemetery **turn left** on the road in the direction of Montauban. Pause for a moment. The high ground ahead of you, just in

**Soldiers of the 9th (Scottish) Division return from the fighting at Longueval.**

front of the village, is where the main German support trench known as Montauban Alley ran. It was the final objective of the 18th (Eastern) and 30th Division on 1st July, and was captured by the late morning. With no reserves to bring up, the survivors did not make any further advances across what was then open ground and merely dug in. The line did not move again until the attack of 14th July – two weeks later. **Continue along the road** towards Montauban, it slopes up as it reaches the village. On the outskirts a minor junction is reached, with a large crucifix among some trees on the right. The area near this junction – the fields back towards where you have just walked from – was known as Triangle Point and a small redoubt existed in the German defences. This redoubt was captured by the 17th Manchesters (2nd Pals) on the late morning of 1st July. It then became part of the new front line. Turn sharp left here down a track which at this point is partially sunken. Pause again.

The Dawn Attack of 14th July 1916 was at the time a very unpopular plan with both the French on the right of the line and General Sir Douglas Haig at his forward headquarters in the chateau of Beauquesne. The idea was to move divisions forward in the dark, attack in the half light just before dawn and preceded by only a short – yet

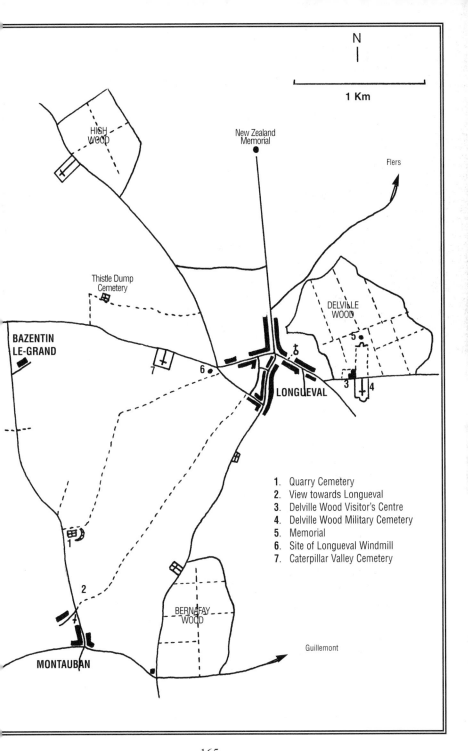

N

1 Km

New Zealand
Memorial

Flers

HIGH
WOOD

Thistle Dump
Cemetery

DELVILLE
WOOD

BAZENTIN
LE-GRAND

7

6

5

3   4

LONGUEVAL

1. Quarry Cemetery
2. View towards Longueval
3. Delville Wood Visitor's Centre
4. Delville Wood Military Cemetery
5. Memorial
6. Site of Longueval Windmill
7. Caterpillar Valley Cemetery

1

2

BERNAFAY
WOOD

Guillemont

MONTAUBAN

fierce – artillery bombardment. A form of creeping barrage (as yet still experimental) would also be used to allow the infantry to move forward with some degree of protection and the whole artillery plan would not be as inflexible as it had been on 1st July. Rawlinson, commanding Fourth Army, and his two Corps commanders for this area – Lieutenant-General H.S. Horne (XV Corps) and Lieutenant-General W.N. Congreve VC (XIII Corps) – were very positive about the whole operation, but Haig felt that such a manoeuvre could not even be implemented on an exercise in peacetime, let alone in current circumstances. After delays and dispute, a plan for an operation on a front from Contalmaison to Longueval was agreed upon, with the main German second line between Bazentin-le-Petit, Longueval and Delville Wood being the overall objective. In some places the new British line and the German second line were over 1,000 yards apart and to shorten the distance over which the attacking troops had to advance the plan

**German map of the Dawn Attack 14 July, 1916.**

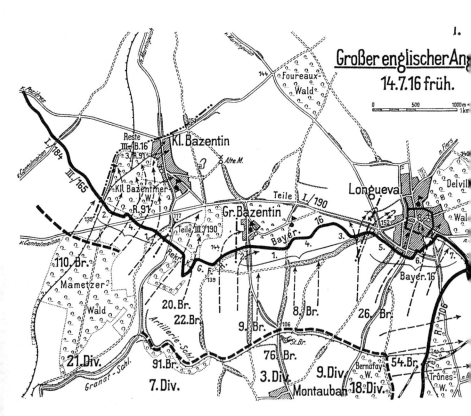

involved 'biting off' large areas of ground between the two lines which the weak German forces around the two Bazentins and Longueval would, indeed could, not contest. This was done on the night of 13th July, and the large valley in which Quarry Cemetery stands was simply swept up by units of the 3rd and 9th (Scottish) Divisions, and new lines were established on the opposite slopes.

The track you are now on was used on 14th July as a brigade boundary by the 9th Division. The 26th Brigade (8th Black Watch, 7th Seaforths, 5th Camerons, 10th Argylls) advanced over the ground on the right of the track. the 27th Brigade (11th and 12th Royal Scots, 6th KOSB, 9th Scottish Rifles) were on the left. The leading battalions from left to right were 9th Scottish Rifles, 11th Royal Scots, 10th Argylls and 8th Black Watch. **Continue along the track**. Longueval is visible in the far distance. As you move further down, Bernafay Wood and the main D.197 road can be seen on the right. After a while a valley is reached; a continuation of the one in which Quarry Cemetery stands. As the track goes down the slope into the valley it becomes sunken and in the summer months the plants and small trees that grow within make progress difficult; walkers must therefore follow it from above, walking where it joins the field and taking care not to damage crops. During the battle the sunken lane was used as a battle headquarters and dugouts started by the German artillery, who had first used the valley, were taken over by the staff of the 9th Division. In the ploughing months a great deal of the Iron Harvest can be found dumped in and around the sunken lane.

Beyond the sunken lane the track improves and can be followed once again in the direction of Longueval. As the rise is reached and Longueval becomes visible ahead, **stop**. This is the area over which the leading waves of 9th (Scottish) Division advanced on 14th July. After

**Pipe band of the Black Watch after the attack on Longueval.**

assembling between Montauban and Bernafay Wood the 26th and 27th Brigades moved up to these advanced positions and attacked the German lines in front of the village. Before them an advanced party of four infantry platoons and two Lewis guns had come forward to give covering fire and screen the final assembly on the reverse slope before the village. Marker tapes had been laid out by Royal Engineers to show attacking battalions the way forward and the whole operation of laying out tapes, bringing up the covering party and main body of troops was '... carried out without a sound and without the least hitch'[1]. All units moved at zero hour, 3.20am, following as far as possible the artillery barrage which, although short, was seen to be quite effective. The 9th Scottish Rifles on the far left were first to enter the German lines around the old Longueval windmill, closely followed by other battalions of 27th Brigade. Opposite the Jocks in this operation was the 16th (Bavarian) Infantry Regiment from Munich. The second battalion of this regiment held the line from Bazentin-le-Grand to Longueval and saw the 9th (Scottish) Division moving forward:

> '... in the early hours the enemy attacked mainly on the front held by the 5th and 6th companies, on the south-west and south-east of Longueval. As soon as the 5th Coy sentries noticed the approach of the enemy, the alarm was raised and the men stormed out of their cover. Lt Thurnreiter on the right wing fired a star-shell. By its light the close columns of plucky Scottish troops could be seen approaching the remains of the wire entanglements, flame-throwers to the fore.'[2]

On the left of the Scots, the 3rd Division was held up attacking Bazentin-le-Grand, so units of the 26th Brigade were pushed forward, reached their objectives around Sloane Street and Dover Street, and moved to help the 27th Brigade push on to the main body of Longueval. By 6.15am units of both brigades were in the village. However strong German counter-attacks then started and the determined Bavarians pushed the troops back to a line that ran from Clareges Street in the western part of Longueval to Princes Street, the main ride through Delville Wood. By midday most of Longueval had still not fallen, and the South African Brigade, itself the third brigade in the 9th Division, was brought up to continue the fighting and push the Germans out of Longueval and Delville Wood.

**Continue along the track**; as it comes into the outskirts of Longueval it becomes partially sunken again. When the track ends, it joins a metalled road, known as Sloane Street on British trench maps. **Turn right** here into the village. At the end **turn left** and follow the main D.197 into the centre of Longueval. In the main square are two small cafes, serving the usual refreshments but no food. Opposite is the fine village war memorial and round the corner is the church, outside of which is a British 9.45-inch trench mortar, now next to a large green bottle bank. **In the centre of the village turn right** on the D.20 following signs to Ginchy, Guillemont and Delville Wood. Continue on this road to the outskirts of the village, where the road forks at a civilian cemetery and **turn left** on the Ginchy road. Delville Wood is found a few hundred yards further along, on the left. The car park and visitors' centre is seen first, where refreshments, souvenirs, maps and books can be bought. There are picnic tables, and it also boasts very good toilets! The main museum, memorial and military cemetery are located further up from the visitors' centre.

The South African Brigade had joined the 9th (Scottish) Division after the Battle of Loos, when the division had suffered such heavy casualties that several of the Scottish battalions were disbanded. The four battalions of South African infantry, which included one kilted battalion, had themselves been formed from several regiments which had fought against the Germans in South-West Africa in 1914/15. Ironically, many of these men had fought against the British in the Boer War of 1899-1902, but by 1914 saw Germany as the greater enemy in Africa. After the entry of 9th Division into Longueval on 14th July the South African Brigade entered Delville Wood early the next morning, when they captured the southern edge and cleared it of Germans. A further attack that day drove the Germans out of all but the north-west corner of the wood. The South Africans dug in, and fought off counter-attack after counter-attack over the next few days. The trench lines-often just connected shell holes – moved backwards and forwards, until the South Africans were relieved and moved out of Delville Wood on the night of 19th/20th July. Only three officers and 140 other ranks from the whole brigade made it out unscathed. Casualties were appalling; the dead alone among the four battalions numbered 766. The ferocious nature of the fighting can be realised in that of this number, only 113 have known graves today. One of the South Africans, Cpl Hermann Bloom, wrote to his parents giving a graphic account of the action at Delville Wood:

'It was no 'tea party'; we had only started when we were deluged with gas and tear shells, whizz-bangs, Jack Johnsons, and all the diabolical stuff that Krupps ever invented. we got orders to advance. It absolutely rained lead... we still went on until we came to close quarters... it was terrible; there was no quarter given.

When we went into the wood the growth was so dense you

**Memorial to the South African Brigade in Delville Wood soon after completion.**

could hardly see ten yards in front of you, but before long there was neither a bough nor a leaf left; the bare trees stood out riddled with lead, and the wood was a mass of dead and wounded – it was awful!'[3]

Delville Wood remained the most significant and costly action the South African Brigade ever fought on the Western Front. Just as other Commonwealth nations selected areas of the 'old front line' as sites for their national memorial, the South Africans chose Delville Wood and acquired the ground at the end of the war. By then a few wooden memorials to the tremendous losses here had been erected, but the South Africans set about making a more permanent form of memorial, which can be found in the wood today. The memorial is a large archway flanked by two walls and a stone of remembrance. Beyond is Delville Wood Museum, open every day except Mondays. It has some interesting exhibits and photographs on the history of South African forces in all twentieth century conflicts, plus some fine bronzes depicting South African men in battle. The one for the Delville Wood action captures well the haunted look on the men's faces as they came out of the wood. This is an essential part of any visit to the area.

It is possible to walk all through the wood, along the various rides that crisscross it; all were given names in 1916 and these are perpetuated on marker stones at the junction of each ride. The last surviving tree from the pre-war wood can be found to the rear of the museum, and opposite it a cleared trench line disappears among the scrub. If followed it will bring you to the site of the South African Brigade's battle headquarters, marked by a stone obelisk. On warm summer days, the cool peaceful glades in the wood belie the horror of the fighting that took place here in July 1916.

**Returning to the main road** that borders the wood, the military cemetery is located opposite.

## DELVILLE WOOD MILITARY CEMETERY

The cemetery was made after the war by concentrating isolated graves and smaller cemeteries in the area; among those moved in were some cemeteries from as far away as Curlu and Courcelette. Today there are 5,236 British graves, 152 South African, eighty-one Australian, twenty-nine Canadian, nineteen New Zealand and three whose unit is not known. Of these 3,590 are unknown, and there are twenty-six Special Memorials. Of the 152 South African graves, seventy are unknowns, the majority from the 1st South African Infantry. The most senior South African buried in the cemetery is Major Harry Herbert Allen Gee (VII-L-5) of the 2nd South African Infantry. Gee took over

**Delville Wood Military Cemetery.**

command of the battalion when the commanding officer had been wounded in Delville Wood; he was hit himself soon afterwards. Before the war Gee had worked on the railways in South Africa, and had commanded the Uitenhage Volunteer Rifles. He served as a Captain in South-West Africa, was promoted to Major in France and was aged forty-eight when he died here on 19th July 1916.

A Somme Victoria Cross winner is also buried in the cemetery. Sgt Albert Gill (IV-C-3) was serving with the 1st KRRC when his battalion attacked Prince's Street in Delville Wood at 7am on 27th July 1916. A former Birmingham Post Office worker, Sgt Gill took command of his men after heavy officer casualties, and organised bombing parties to protect the recently captured German lines. Part of his citation reads:

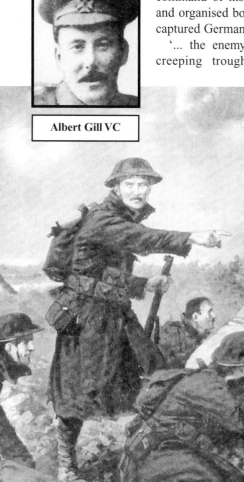

Albert Gill VC

'... the enemy nearly surrounded his men by creeping trough the thick undergrowth, and commenced sniping at about twenty yards range. Although it was almost certain death, Sgt Gill stood boldly up in order to direct the fire of his men. He was killed almost at once, but not before he had shown his men where the enemy were, and this enabled them to hold up their advance.'[4]

Gill was thirty-six when he was killed, and was the fourth man to be awarded a VC for bravery in Delville Wood. Many of the other graves in the cemetery come from other areas of the Somme battlefield, especially Pozières and High Wood. One of these is a Special Memorial to Second Lieutenant Nevill Lindsay Young (Sp Mem A-9). Young was a junior subaltern in the 2nd Royal Sussex Regiment when he was killed near Wood

Lane trench at High Wood in August 1916; his father was a Major-General who was also Colonel of the Regiment.

Leaving the military cemetery **turn left** and return to the centre of Longueval by the road. In the centre of the village **go straight on**, following signs to Bazentin-le-Petit on the main D.20. Past the outskirts of Longueval a cross roads is reached. Ahead is the continuation of the D.20, to the right the D.107 to High Wood and Martinpuich, and left the beginning of Sloane Street. **Turn left** onto Sloane Street, then **first right** onto a minor track past a calvary. Longueval Windmill was once located in the field behind the calvary.

The track becomes sunken at first, and further on there are good views to the left over the expanse of ground around Montauban over which British troops advanced on 14th July and the area you have previously walked. **Continue on** to a cross-roads of tracks, **then stop**. The 3rd Division attacked across this ground on 14th July. On the left 9th Brigade moved forward with the 12th West Yorkshires and 13th King's Liverpool regiment leading. Both battalions captured all their objectives, but between them lost over 500 casualties. On the right 8th Brigade advanced; among them the 8th East Yorkshires and 7th King's Shropshire Light Infantry. The author Frederick Manning was serving with the latter unit, and took part in the fighting; it was later recounted through his fictional character, Bourne, in *Her Privates We*. Casualties in these two units amounted to over 400 each; the commanding officer of the 8th East Yorks was wounded in the fighting. German machine-gun fire was heavy during this attack, but the 1st Northumberland Fusiliers, in support of the 9th Brigade, pushed on and successfully entered Bazentin-Le-Grand village over the rise to the right of where you are walking; it cost them over 200 men killed, wounded and missing. In recent times this track has been improved, and now slopes downhill to Quarry Cemetery and your vehicle.

READING LIST

Digby, P.K.A.   *Pyramids and Poppies: The 1st SA Brigade in Libya, France and Flanders 1915-1919* (Ashanti 1991)

Manning, F.   *Her Privates We* (Peter Davies 1929)

Talbot Kelly, R.B. *A Subaltern's Odyssy* (Kimber 1980)

Uys, I.   *Delville Wood* (Uys Publishers 1983)

Uys, I.   *Longueval* (Uys Publishers 1986)

# HIGH WOOD

STARTING POINT: **Bazentin-le-Petit Communal Cemetery Extension**
DURATION: **3½ hours**
WALK SUMMARY: **A pleasant, largely cross-country walk which gives the walker a good impression of the ground around High Wood where fighting took place for over two months between July and September 1916.**

*Bazentin-le-Petit Communal Cemetery Extension is reached from Bazentin village via a minor road (Rue Neuve) which is almost directly opposite the church; it is signposted with the usual green CWGC sign. It is advisable to park your vehicle either on the grass outside the adjacent French local cemetery or in the nearby quarry.*

**Bazentin-le-Petit village, 1916.**

This area of ground was captured during the so-called Dawn Attack of 14th July 1916 (see Dawn Attack Walk). Bazentin-le-Petit village fell to men of the 7th Division who then advanced eastwards, taking the area around Bazentin quarry where you are now. Parties were pushed up to the high ground beyond, but came under fire from Bazentin Windmill- not quite visible here but visited later in the walk. However, after a short firefight this area was also taken and from there the view across to High Wood was wide open.

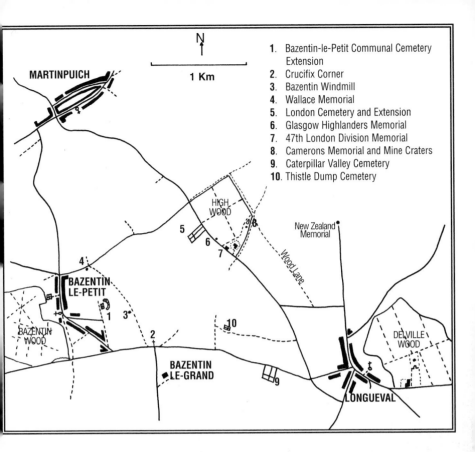

# BAZENTIN-LE-PETIT COMMUNAL CEMETERY EXTENSION

This battlefield cemetery was begun after the capture of Bazentin in July 1916, and used until December of that year. Many of the men were killed in the fighting towards High Wood and Martinpuich, but a number died of wounds in the various RAMC Field Ambulances which were established in the quarry to the rear of the cemetery, now overgrown. Many men wounded at High Wood were brought to this quarry; among them poet and author Robert Graves who was wounded with the 2nd Royal Welsh Fusiliers in July 1916. His experiences were related in *Goodbye To All That*. A further fifty graves were added to the cemetery after the war, and today there are 180 British, five Canadian and one Australian. Of these fifty-three are of unknown soldiers, and there are fifty-nine Special Memorials to men – largely from the 1st Northamptonshires – whose graves were destroyed in later fighting. A large portion of the graves are men from the 50th (Northumbrian)

Division who fell in the fighting around Martinpuich-High Wood; men from northern territorial units. The 1st Northamptonshires are well represented, both among the graves and the Special Memorials already mentioned; among them are two company commanders from the battalion killed near the Switch Line at High Wood – Captain J.G. Clayton (Spec Mem C.17) who died on 20th August aged twenty-one, and Captain A.E. Sewell DSO (E-3) who died three days earlier. An interesting and intriguing grave can be found at A-8; the stone indicates this soldier was from the Royal Jersey Militia. This regiment had three battalions of infantry at the outbreak of war in 1914, but never served overseas as a unit. However, it provided a full company of men in March 1915 to the 7th Royal Irish Rifles in the 16th (Irish) Division.

Leaving the cemetery via the gate, **turn left** onto the **cart track** and a few yards on the left is the main entrance to the local French civilian cemetery; go in. This is BAZENTIN COMMUNAL CEMETERY on the original site of the pre-1914 local cemetery; two burials were made in August 1916. These were Lieutenant L.S.H. Griffin of the 10th Gloucestershire Regiment and RSM W. Pearce of the 10th Loyal North Lancashire Regiment. Both men were killed near High Wood; some locals in Bazentin say that the bodies of these soldiers were found by French civilians after the war and brought back to the village cemetery for re-burial.

Leave the cemetery by the main entrance and again **turn left onto the cart track**. Bazentin village is over on your right. **Continue** along the track past the quarry on the left, and where the track meets a turning to the right back into Bazentin, ignore this and **continue straight on**. Stay on this track, past some

**Crucifix Corner, Bazentin-le-Petit.**

houses on the right until the track meets the main Contalmaison-Longueval road (D.20). **Turn left** onto the road and continue along it until a junction signposted for Bazentin-le-Grand is reached; a crucifix among some trees is opposite this junction on the left. This was one of a number of places known as Crucifix Corner on the Somme battlefield. A cavalry charge was made towards High Wood on 14th July 1916, and it swept past this junction on its way up to the wood that day. As the fighting continued, Field Ambulances took over the ruins of a farm and former German medical centre in Bazentin-le-Grand; the new farm is visible on the high ground opposite the crucifix. A number of battalion medical officers set up their Regimental Aid Posts in front of this crucifix; it is out of view from the former German positions around High Wood and Longueval. Men were laid on stretchers on the road, and once patched up evacuated via Bazentin-le-Grand for further treatment. The figure of Christ on the crucifix among the trees here is the original; it survived although damaged by shrapnel and bullet fire, which is still visible. In recent years the villagers of Bazentin have taken a great interest in the history of their village and this and several other sites in the area have been restored or repaired; a small flight of access steps have been constructed here.

Leaving the crucifix **turn right**, back towards Bazentin-le-Petit. A few yards on the right a cart track appears, going gradually uphill. Follow this track as it climbs the high ground to a visible area of trees and scrub to the left of the track. This scrub covered mound is the site of Bazentin Windmill, and from here there are commanding views towards High Wood and Longueval to the right. Battalion after battalion attacked across the ground before you, with many thousands of men losing their lives in this relatively small corner of the Somme battlefield. The fighting around High Wood continued from the first attacks on 14th July right through until it was captured on 15th September. During those two months almost every type of warfare was tried- a cavalry charge, full frontal infantry assaults, gas bombardments, flame thrower attacks, machine-gun barrages, and finally tanks.

The ruins of the Bazentin Windmill were used right throughout the battle; artillery observers watched the fighting from this vantage point and directed the guns. Signallers also established posts here- among them Frank Richards of 2nd Royal Welsh Fusiliers who later related his experiences at High Wood in the classic Great War memoir, *Old Soldiers Never Die*. Scan the horizon towards the wood from left to right; the spire of Martinpuich church can be seen, then High Wood itself, the ground to the right of the wood was where the cavalry charge on 14th July ended up, then Longueval village and church spire, finally the large Caterpillar Valley British Cemetery is visible on the right.

**Continue along the track** as it veers towards the north of Bazentin. Eventually it comes out in a partially sunken lane. On the left is a bank and among the trees a wooden crucifix mounted on a small cairn of stones. This is a private memorial erected after the Great War by the family of Captain Houston Stewart Hamilton Wallace. Wallace was an officer in the 10th Worcestershire Regiment and was killed in the area north-east from the memorial on 22nd July 1916. On this day his battalion made an unsuccessful attack towards High Wood; Wallace's D Company suffering heavily from machine-gun and shrapnel fire. Born at Birkenhead in 1894, Wallace was educated at Fettes and Merton College, joining the Worcestershire Regiment in November 1914. He served in France from June 1915, first at Ypres and then the Somme. Posted missing after his death near High Wood, Captain Wallace's body was never found – today his name can be found on the Thiepval Memorial. His parents having died before the war, his aunt came to Bazentin in the early 1920s and selected an area of ground for a memorial close to where he was known to have died. This memorial took the form of a large wooden crucifix, with a mahogany figure of Christ. It survived for many years in this often exposed position, until the cross came down during a storm in the early 1980s. Rescued by a local villager, it remained in this man's garage until 1994 when the people of Bazentin along with the Western Front Association paid for the memorial to be restored.

**Memorial to Captain H S H Wallace.**

From the memorial **join the metalled minor road** running east towards High Wood from Bazentin-le-Petit. Stay on this road and continue until the road dips down into a minor valley running to the right of the road. Stop here. The road you are on was known as

Upper Road to British troops, and from here many attacks were made towards Martinpuich and a long German trench known as the Switch Line or Switch Trench. Switch Trench ran from Martinpuich to the north-western corner of High Wood and commanded the ground you are now walking over. The valley to the right of Upper Road was Death Valley; originally a German battery position prior to 1st July, all attacks from Bazentin were made across this ground. After several operations, and many casualties, the trenches – or often just connected shell holes – were on the reverse slope of the valley towards the wood and among the broken trees in the south-east corner. It was from these positions that the final attack on High Wood was made on 15th September 1916. By this time the ground all around where you are now was a vast moonscape of shell holes and shallow trenches, made worse by the increasing rainfall and cold weather. Now **continue** along the road until it meets the Martinpuich-Longueval road (D.107) at the western corner of High Wood. **Turn right onto the road**. The wood now borders the road on the left. Continue on the D.107 until the military cemetery is reached on the right, a few hundred yards further on.

## LONDON CEMETERY & EXTENSION, HIGH WOOD

By the end of the Somme the only battlefield cemetery close to High Wood was London Cemetery which contained the graves of 101 British soldiers buried here in a large shell hole after the September 1916 operations. The majority of these graves were men who died in the final attack on High Wood when it was captured by the 47th (London) Division assisted by tanks, being used for the first time. Of these graves two men from the 1/19th London Regiment are of particular interest; RSM A.F. Ridout (A-9) was the most senior Warrant Officer in the battalion killed on 15th September. Captain David Henderson (A-13) died the same day, aged twenty-seven, and was the son of the Labour Party leader, Arthur Henderson.

Going through this small 'regimental cemetery' one passes under some arches into the London Cemetery Extension. This was added in the late 1920s, when the many isolated graves and burial sites all over the Somme battlefield were brought into a number of larger cemeteries, this being one. Graves from other parts of the Western Front were also brought here, including from as far away as the Aisne. Burials continued until well after the Second World War, including a number of men from that very war- now to be found in a separate plot behind the Cross of Sacrifice. The vast majority of the 3,769 Great War graves in London Cemetery Extension are unknown.

Leaving the cemetery by the main gate, **go right onto the main road** again and continue along the edge of High Wood. Along this edge of the wood there are three memorials, all of which should be visited:

## GLASGOW HIGHLANDERS MEMORIAL

This is a private memorial to the 1/9th Battalion Highland Light Infantry (Glasgow Highlanders) erected in 1972 by author Alex Aitken, whose father served in the battalion. The Glasgow Highlanders were a Territorial Force battalion raised in Glasgow, and was one of the first such units to go to France in 1914. In the fighting around High Wood, 192 members of the battalion were killed; this cairn is made up of 192 stones – each representing one of the casualties. The height of the memorial is also the average height of a Glasgow Highlanders' recruit.

## 20TH ROYAL FUSILIERS MEMORIAL

Easily missed, this little plaque alongside a small tree was planted here by Don Price in the mid-1980s. An old soldier of the 20th Royal Fusiliers (Public Schools Battalion), Price fought at High Wood with his unit in July 1916, when they suffered heavy casualties. The 2nd Royal Welsh Fusiliers – a regular battalion -disdainfully nick-named these Public Schoolboys the 'chocolate soldiers' as their parcels from home frequently contained large amounts of chocolate!

## 47TH (LONDON) DIVISION MEMORIAL

A much earlier memorial, it commemorates the battalions of the 47th (London) London Division who successfully took High Wood on 15th September 1916. The 47th was a territorial division which had been in France since March 1915, and had previously fought at Loos and on

Vimy Ridge. Its battalions had a very high reputation, and despite suffering severe losses in the High Wood fighting, captured both the wood and Switch Trench with the aid of tanks, used here for the first time. Having a strong Old Comrades Association, the division erected this permanent memorial which was unveiled in September 1925. Another can be found in Martinpuich (see Butte

**An old soldier of the London Regiment stands before the memorial to the 47th (London) Division before its unveiling in 1927. Due to problems with the foundations, it was completely rebuilt in 1996.**

de Warlencourt Walk). Due to continual problems with the foundations of the memorial, it was rebuilt and re-dedicated in 1996 and bears only a slight resemblance to its original form. From this spot there are spectacular views across the ground you have just walked, and (from left to right) the church spires of Longueval, Montauban, Bazentin and Martinpuich can be clearly seen.

**Continue along the main road**. Further on, past the entrance to modern house in the wood, **turn left** at the southern corner of High Wood and take a minor road that borders the treeline. About two thirds of the way along is a memorial to the 1st Cameron Highlanders. The 1st Camerons was a regular army battalion which had been in France since August 1914, and had fought in many of the earlier battles of the war. It took part in various engagements around High Wood from late July to early September 1916; in one attack alone at this corner of the wood over 240 men in the battalion became casualties. There are water-filled mine craters to the rear of the memorial, but they are on private property and can only be seen from a distance. These date from 3rd September 1916 and were laid by men of the 178th Tunnelling Company Royal Engineers as part of one of the attacks made by 1st Cameron Highlanders.

From the memorial **continue** along the track to the north-eastern corner of the wood. From here there are good views to the left towards

**A modern aerial view of High Wood, looking north to Martinpuich. London Cemetery can be seen to the left.** *John Giles*

Le Sars and Eaucourt L'Abbaye, and the Butte de Warlencourt can also be seen on clear days. To the right far distance the church spire of Flers is visible. To the immediate right is Longueval and Delville Wood. This is all ground over which the Somme campaign continued after the capture of High Wood. At this corner of the wood **follow a minor road** that runs towards Longueval; it is metalled at first and later becomes a cart track. **Follow this route** for a couple of hundred yards and then **stop**. This minor road was known as Wood Lane, and was an area much fought over in the 1916 fighting for High Wood. Heavily defended by the Germans with the nearby Wood Lane trench, one early attack here by the 1st Royal West Kents on 22nd July 1916 resulted in heavy casualties as the battalion was skylined coming over the crest of ground to the right of the track as you walk towards Longueval. All the officers fell leading their men forward, and total losses in the battalion numbered 421.

**Stay on the track**; further along Wood Lane becomes sunken and then it reaches another minor metalled road. **Go right** here onto the road, and follow until it reaches the D.107 Martinpuich-Longueval road. Here **go left** in the direction of Longueval itself, and follow D.107 downhill. Further on there are some concrete pylons where a metalled track on the right meets the road; **take this track** which follows a valley. Caterpillar Valley Cemetery is on the high ground to the left; High Wood is back over to your right. Stay on this route, as it follows the valley until a military cemetery is reached.

THISTLE DUMP CEMETERY

Begun in August 1916 while the battle for High Wood still raged, and used until February 1917 latterly by Australian units, this isolated cemetery has 107 British, thirty-seven New Zealand and thirty-six Australian burials. Over fifty graves were brought in from all over the Somme after the war, including a number of men from Pals units who died at Serre on 1st July 1916. German burials from 1916 and the Spring of 1918 have been left in the cemetery. Charles Frederick Foster (B-20) was a thirty-four year old subaltern in the 2nd Battalion Royal Sussex Regiment who had come from Natal, South Africa, to enlist. He was killed in the fighting around High Wood on 9th September 1916. Second Lieutenant John Handyside (E-19) was a former philosophy lecturer at Liverpool University, who was killed in October 1916 with the 2nd Liverpool Pals. Many of the New Zealand graves here are men who died fighting near High Wood, and include a number of men from the New Zealand Field Artillery who had their guns in this valley after the capture of the wood.

Leaving the cemetery, **turn right** outside the gate and continue along the track. A short distance further up the track goes to the left uphill towards the main Longueval-Bazentin road (D.20). Follow to the road and **turn right** in the direction of Bazentin. Staying on the D.20 for a while, Crucifix Corner is passed again on the right. Back on the outskirts of Bazentin-le-Petit the road junction leading to the village is reached. A minor track used earlier in the walk is on the right before the road; this should be followed back to Bazentin-le-Petit Communal Cemetery and your vehicle.

READING LIST

Aiken, A.      *Courage Past – A Duty Done* (Glasgow 1971)
Eyre, G.       *Somme Harvest* (Jarrold 1938)
Graves, R.     *Goodbye To All That* (many paperback edns)
Hodson, J.L. *Return To The Wood* (Gollanz 1955)
Norman, T.   *The Hell They Called High Wood* (William Kimber 1984)
Richards, F.   *Old Soldiers Never Die* (Faber 1933)

# THE TANK WALK : LONGUEVAL-GINCHY-FLERS

STARTING POINT:  **Delville Wood car park, Longueval**
DURATION:  **4 hours**
WALK SUMMARY:  **This walk covers some of the ground around Flers where tanks were used for the first time on 15th September 1916. It also takes in some of the fighting north of Longueval and around Ginchy.**

*Delville Wood is well sign-posted from Longueval village. Park your vehicle in the car park of Delville Wood visitors' centre; there are toilets, picnic facilities and a shop and tea room here.*

Leave the car park area and move out onto the main Longueval-Ginchy road, **turning left** in the direction of Ginchy. Moving along the southern edge of Delville Wood you will pass the area of the museum and memorial, and on the right, Delville Wood Cemetery. These are not part of the walk, but for more information see the Dawn Attack Walk elsewhere in this book.

Continuing along the road, eventually the wood will fall away to the left, and fields will open up on both sides. Go **past the water tower**, staying on the road for Ginchy. The fields on the left were the site of trenches known as Hop Alley and Ale Alley where heavy fighting took place after the initial fighting in Delville Wood in July 1916. Even by 11th September the 55th (West Lancashire) Division was still fighting over this ground with a full frontal attack that again failed. The British front line on 15th September 1916 – the day tanks were first used – ran along this road; it was known as Pilsen Lane trench. Tank D1 advanced from near the area of the current water tower, followed by men of 6th KOYLI. However, this tank was struck by a shell and could advance no further; the men of 6th KOYLI came under heavy machine-gun fire, but took the German positions at the point of the bayonet. They moved on and linked up with the Guards Division on their right.

Continue along the Ginchy road; further along it bends to the right. About a hundred yards past this bend **a track** appears **on the left**, following trees bordering a wired-off field. **Follow this track** in roughly a northern direction. As you go along, there are good views to the left towards Delville Wood where men of 6th KOYLI and other battalions of the 14th (Light) Division advanced on 15th September. Another tank attached to the Guards Division crossed this track on that day, also advancing on Ale Alley trench. However, the rough ground

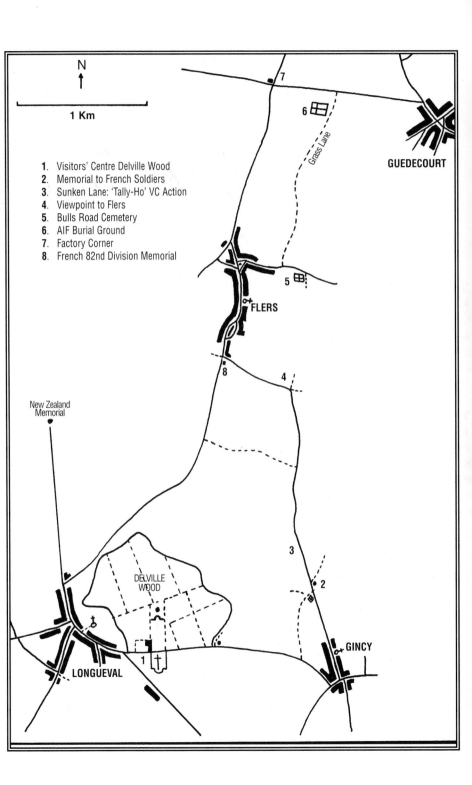

N

1 Km

1. Visitors' Centre Delville Wood
2. Memorial to French Soldiers
3. Sunken Lane: 'Tally-Ho' VC Action
4. Viewpoint to Flers
5. Bulls Road Cemetery
6. AIF Burial Ground
7. Factory Corner
8. French 82nd Division Memorial

GUEDECOURT

Grass Lane

7

6

5

FLERS

8

4

New Zealand
Memorial

3

2

DELVILLE
WOOD

1

LONGUEVAL

GINCY

**A ditched Mark I male tank (6pdr guns) during the Flers operations, 15 September 1916.** *Geoff Bridger*

caused it to ditch. Flers is now visible in the distance to the north from this track. Stay on the track; it bends to the right further up and passes the modern Ginchy civilian cemetery on the right. Just past the cemetery the track comes out onto the main Ginchy-Flers road. **Turn left** here in the direction of Flers. About a hundred or so yards further up on the right is a French Memorial among some trees. Stop. This memorial is one of two in this area that commemorates the fighting between the French and Germans here on 26th September 1914. This one is dedicated to two French soldiers who fell in the action near Flers and Ginchy: Sergeant Georges Lejoindre, aged thirty-six, and Sergeant Georges Pfister, aged thirty-eight and winner of the Medaille Militaire and Croix de Guerre. Both men were members of the 18th Territorial Infantry Regiment. Although well kept by Souvenir Francais, it is a rarely visited private memorial.

Continue along the Flers road. Beyond the memorial the road becomes sunken. **Stop in the sunken part**, near the pylons. Pint Trench ran along the left hand edge of the road you are on. On 15th September the 1st Guards Brigade attacked from Ginchy towards this ground. Advancing on the left to the sunken lane, the men of 2nd and 3rd Coldstream Guards were held up by machine-guns in both Pint Trench and in the sunken lane. Coldstreams fell in droves, but the commanding officer of 3rd Coldstream, Lieutenant-Colonel John Vaughan Campbell

DSO, realised that a critical moment had come in the advance. He jumped up and rallied his men with a blast from a hunting horn he always carried with him. A regular officer who had been in the Coldstream Guards since 1896 and was awarded the DSO for gallantry in the Boer War, before 1914 Campbell had been master of a hunt in Shropshire. Just one blast from the horn was enough to inspire his men forward and the sunken lane was rushed and taken by fierce hand-to-hand fighting. The advance now continued towards Lesboeufs, and Campbell and his men went on to capture all their objectives. For his bravery that day Campbell was awarded the Victoria Cross in October 1916; he also became known as the 'Tally Ho VC' in the popular press. Campbell's later career saw him commanding 3rd Guards Brigade, and after the war he became ADC to

The 'Tally-Ho VC' attacking the Sunken Lane near Ginchy on 15 September 1916.

King George V. During the Second World War he served in the Home Guard until his death in 1944.

**Continue** along the Flers road. Exceptional views are gained from this road; to the left and right, and back towards Ginchy as well. It reaches a high point with a line of young trees bordering the road on the left. From here Flers can now be seen to the north-west. Good views back to Ginchy and Delville Wood can be obtained. On a very clear day, eleven church spires are visible from this spot – one of the highest points in this part of the battlefield. In September 1916 the infamous Switch Trench ran across the road here; this was the trench that ran from High Wood, which is in the distance to the left. On 15th September the position was defended by the 14th Bavarian Regiment and assaulted by men of the 42nd Brigade, 14th (Light) Division along with tank D5. This tank passed across Switch Trench and eventually on towards Guedecourt – also visible from here on the right – but was hit and set on fire just short of the village. The 42nd Brigade eventually took up positions east of Flers and beat off a German counter-attack on the evening of the 15th.

**A Mark I female tank (machine-guns) ditched near Flers, 15 September 1916.** *Geoff Bridger*

Again **continue along the road**, which bends sharply to the left. **Stop** at this point and look towards Flers. The 41st Division advanced across this ground on 15th September. A New Army Division, the 41st had only been in France since May 1916, and Flers was their first major action. Flers Avenue trench ran along the road towards the village and was attacked by the 122nd Brigade on 15th September – comprising 18th KRRC (Arts and Crafts Bn), 15th Hampshires (Portsmouth Pals), 11th Royal West Kents (Lewisham Bn), 12th East Surreys (Bermondsey Bn) – and assisted by two tanks: D14 and D17. D14 hit rough ground near Flers and was forced to ditch. The other, D17, went in with the infantry at Flers Avenue, but was hit by shell fire and immobilised. Meanwhile the men of 122 Brigade pushed on, were joined by further tanks and advanced to Bulls Road which ran east from the northern tip of Flers. This was the furthest extent of the attack here that day.

Follow the road downhill to a road junction on the Longueval-Flers road. Turn right here into Flers and follow the main road past war memorial, church and farms to the centre of the village. On a green set among some trees and bushes is one of the finest memorials on the Somme – to the 41st Division. It is a copy of the Royal Fusiliers memorial in Holborn; possibly because there were two Royal Fusilier battalions in the division. The soldier, in full battle order, looks down the main road of Flers where men of the division and tank D16 advanced on 15th September; this led to the famous newspaper headline proclaiming that tanks were advancing through Flers 'followed by the whole of the British Army'. The 41st went on to fight in many later battles of the war, and also served in Italy, but the Flers action remained among the most costly – yet successful – operations in which they fought, and is probably the reason the division's Old Comrades Association chose to erect the memorial here in the early 1920s. From the memorial take **a minor road to the right** of the statue, passing an imposing house on the right. At the end **turn right** onto what is Bulls Road and follow this out of the village, downhill through a sunken section, to Bulls Road Cemetery.

**Memorial to 41st Division, Flers.**

*Frank & Lou Stockdale*

**The ruins of Flers, 15 September 1916.**

## BULLS ROAD CEMETERY

Named after the road you have just walked down, the cemetery was begun on 19th September 1916 after the capture of Flers. It was used until March 1917, latterly by units of the Australian Imperial Force (AIF). The original burials were 154 in number, and now form Plots I and II. All the other graves were brought in after the war from the surrounding battlefield. Today Bulls Road Cemetery contains the graves of 485 British burials, with 148 Australian, 120 New Zealand and two whose unit is not known. The unknown burials among them number 296, and there are fifteen Special Memorials. There are several graves here of men from 122nd Brigade, killed on 15th September

**Bulls Road, Flers, September 1916.**

1916, and in particular a large number of men from the Lewisham Battalion – the 11th Royal West Kents. Many of the AIF graves are by the gate as you go into the cemetery and are from the Winter of 1916/17 when the Australians held the line in front of Ligny, and around Guedecourt, on the eastern edges of the 1916 Somme battlefield. In the poor conditions cases of trench foot were among the highest of the war.

190

One AIF man buried here was Gunner John Delo (III-K-25) of 11th Brigade Australian Field Artillery. His parents in Kilkenny, South Australia, named their house 'Flers' after the place where their son was buried; one wonders if they ever made the long journey to see it?

Leaving the cemetery follow the neatly cut grass track down to the metalled road – Bulls Road – and **turn left** towards Flers, following it downhill. Just before the road becomes sunken on the outskirts of the village, a metalled **track appears on the right; follow this**. Another cemetery – AIF Burial Ground – is now visible in the distance. In 1916 this track was known as Grass Lane on British maps. On 15th September tank D9 advanced across the ground here to further German positions known as Box and Cox and captured them. However, like many other tanks that day it found itself in an exposed position and came under shell fire which eventually put the tank out of action. The 41st Division's advance ended here on the 15th, and the lines stabilised in front of Guedecourt until the village finally fell on 26th September. During the Winter of 1916/17, the AIF used Grass Lane as a route to the trenches around Guedecourt and in front of Ligny. This track has been vastly improved and gives better access to AIF Burial Ground which is soon reached.

## AIF BURIAL GROUND, FLERS

This cemetery takes its name from the Australian Imperial Force (AIF); the official name given to the Australian army in the Great War. AIF units held the line near here during the Winter of 1916/17, and began a burial ground for their dead in November 1916; it continued in use until early 1917. Like many Somme cemeteries it was greatly enlarged after the war, and graves were brought in from all over the battlefield. Today there are 2,811 British burials, 402 Australian, eighty-four New Zealand, sixty-eight Canadian and twenty-seven South African. There are also twenty-six Special Memorials, and 163 French graves. Many graves of men whose units and actions are covered in the scope of this walk are buried here. Among them is a very early tank crew grave; Sergeant R.B. Peabody (III-J-12) of the 4th ('D') Battalion who died on 16th September 1916. A notable grave moved into the cemetery after the last war is that of Lieutenant-Colonel Charles William Reginald Duncombe, Earl Feversham (III-L). He will be dealt with later in the walk, but his grave should be seen before proceeding further. He fell near Flers on 15th September, while leading his battalion, 21st KRRC (Yeoman's Rifles). Second Lieutenant Ernest Shepherd (XV-J-17), whose diaries were published some years ago under the title *A Sergeant-Major's War*, is also buried in this cemetery.

Having served in the ranks of the 1st Dorsetshires for many years, he was commissioned into the 5th Battalion and killed on 11th January 1917. A 1918 VC winner is close to the main entrance: Sergeant Harold Jackson (XV-A-21/30) of the 7th East Yorkshire Regiment won his Victoria Cross in the March 1918 offensive. He was killed in the British offensive of August 1918.

Leave the cemetery and turn left back onto Grass Lane, following it to the main Guedecourt road (D.11). Turn left here and continue until a cross-roads is reached. This was known as Factory Corner during the war. One of the battalions that attacked Flers on 15th September was the 21st KRRC (Yeoman's Rifles). This battalion had started life as a 'Farmers Pals Battalion', and was commanded by a well known Yorkshire landowner, the Earl Feversham. Another officer in the battalion later became a British Prime Minister – Anthony Eden. Earl Feversham was killed east of Flers while leading his men forward, but his body had not been immediately recovered. Eden came through the fighting unscathed and due to losses in the battalion became acting adjutant. Some time after the capture of Flers, the 21st KRRC found themselves at Factory Corner and Eden was detailed to look for Earl Feversham's body. After an extensive search it was found on 10th October and he was given a proper burial in fields now close to AIF Burial ground. After the war his family made the site more permanent with a gate and flagstone bearing the Colonel's details. Following the Second World War a lot of these isolated graves were brought into larger cemeteries, and Earl Feversham's was moved to AIF Burial Ground.

The cross-roads at Factory Corner is the junction of the D.74 to Le Sars, the D.10 to Ligny-Thilloy and D.197 to Flers. Take the **D.197 left** to Flers. As you get further towards the village, High Wood is visible in the far distance to the right. Flers is reached after one and a half kilometres. **Continue through the village** on the D.197, known locally as Rue de Bapaume. A bar is passed before the 41st Division memorial, but it is rarely open. Carry on past the memorial through the village towards Longueval. On the outskirts, just past the Ginchy turning, a large grey memorial is visible among the trees up a bank on the left. This is a memorial to the 17th and 18th Territorial Infantry Regiments of the 82nd (Territorial) Division of the French army. Like the one to the two French sergeants north of Ginchy, it commemorates the fighting around Flers, Ginchy and Lesboeufs in September 1914.

Continue towards Longueval. Delville Wood is ahead. About one kilometre out of Flers, the road bends to the right on a corner. Stop and look to the valley on the left. Great War author Ernest Parker took part in an attack across this ground on 16th September, when he was serving as a nineteen year old private in the 10th Durham Light Infantry. In his book *Into Battle 1914-18* he recalled moving up through Delville Wood and being hit by a tornado of German shells as the men moved into the open for the attack. Durhams had already begun to fall, but the battalion kept going into the valley where another bombardment caught them in the open, and the survivors sought shelter in some shell holes. The 10th Durham Light Infantry had been badly cut up in this attack and suffered over 400 casualties.

Carry **on to Longueval**, following the road left past where it borders Delville Wood, and into the village itself. At the **cross-roads** in the centre of Longueval **turn left** following signs for Guillemont, Ginchy and Delville Wood. There are bars on both sides of this junction, which are usually open. On the outskirts of Longueval, take **a left hand** turning at the civilian cemetery, signposted to Delville Wood and Ginchy. The car park back at the visitors' centre is reached a few hundred yards further on.

READING LIST

Eden, A.    *Another World 1897-1917* (Allen Lane 1976)
Parker, E.    *Into Battle 1914-18* (Longmans 1964)
Pidgeon, T.  *The Tanks at Flers* 2 vols (1995)

# BUTTE DE WARLENCOURT

STARTING POINT: **Outside church, Martinpuich**
DURATION: **3 hours**
WALK SUMMARY: **A fairly short walk, suitable for inexperienced walkers, covering some of the infrequently visited ground between Martinpuich, Eaucourt L'Abbaye and the Butte de Warlencourt. This is very much a country walk. It also takes in a rarely visited original 1916 German regimental memorial.**

*Park your vehicle outside Martinpuich church, in the centre of the village; there is plenty of room to pull right off the road. Just by the church on the right is a memorial archway, set back from the road and in front of the Mairie and school.*

Martinpuich was a large village by Somme standards, and was fought over and captured by men of the 15th (Scottish) Division on 15th September 1916, when tanks were used for the first time. However, the memorial archway commemorates the 47th (London) Division; another to the same division exists at High Wood. The 47th operated in this area, and over the ground you are about to walk, after the capture of High Wood also on 15th September. They stayed in this sector until early October and during the Somme fighting the 47th Division lost 296 officers and 7,475 men killed, wounded and missing.

**Modern aerial view from Martinpuich looking east towards the Butte de Warlencourt.** *John Giles*

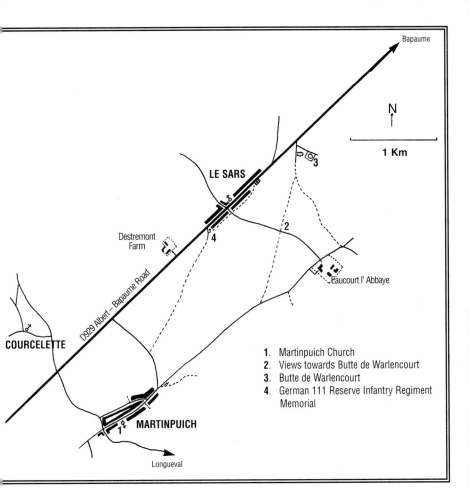

From the memorial **go east towards Eaucourt** along the main road that runs through the village, past farms and houses. On the outskirts of the village the main road turns sharply to the left. Ignore this. Ahead of you are two minor roads, separated by a small brick-built chapel; take the left hand minor road, which is metalled. This minor road leads you out of Martinpuich, and was a main route up to the front lines around the Butte de Warlencourt during the Winter of 1916/17. Many battalions followed this road to the trenches, and often in terrible conditions; the weather during that period was perhaps the worst of the war, with cases of trench foot being especially severe. Temperatures dropped dramatically in January 1917, and life up in the forward zone, where trenches were often connected shell-holes or smashed old

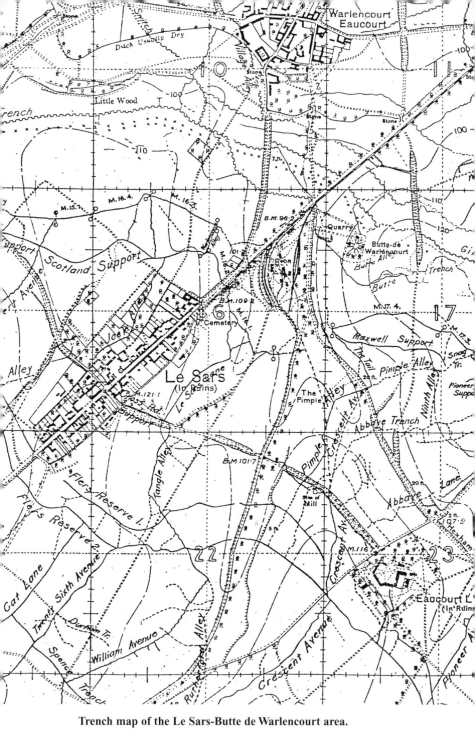

**Trench map of the Le Sars-Butte de Warlencourt area.**

German positions, was miserable to say the least.

Continue along the road. The ground slopes upwards to the left; beyond here is Le Sars, out of site. Ahead is Eaucourt L'Abbaye. The 47th (London) Division fought across this ground in October 1916. The initial attack was on 1st October, when a number of London Regiment battalions from 141 Brigade advanced in the afternoon towards the ruins of Eaucourt L'Abbaye. Eaucourt was a large farm complex, where monks had lived many centuries before. The Germans had turned the extensive grounds, and thick, high walls into a formidable defensive position. The attacking battalions on 1st October – led by the London Irish Rifles and 20th Londons – came under withering machine-gun fire from Eaucourt, but these were eventually silenced by two tanks attached to the brigade. The remains of the farm were then captured by men of the 20th Londons, and a small party of them dug in amongst the rubble. The Division's second objective after Eaucourt was the Butte de Warlencourt. A further attack was made by units of the 140 Brigade on 7th October. This operation was much less successful. The divisional historian recounted with some sadness:

'... the full force of the enemy artillery and machine-gun fire, cleverly sited in depth, so as to bring a withering cross-fire to bear along the western slopes leading up to the Butte and the high ground to the south of it. From across the valley the enemy had magnificent observation of the ground leading to our objective, and made full use of it... not a man turned back, and some got right up under the Butte, but they were not seen again.'[1]

This was one of the first of many attacks to be made on the infamous Butte de Warlencourt.

Continue along the minor road. As it gets nearer to Eaucourt, a track is passed on the right. Ignore this and go on. Further up **on the left**, just before a road sign on the right, another **track** appears. Sometimes a little overgrown, this is the old light railway track that once ran from Martinpuich to the Butte de Warlencourt. Although at places the track is difficult, **follow it** in the direction of the Butte. This track was again one used by units coming up to the front line area around Le Sars and the Butte. Further along, the buildings of modern Eaucourt can be seen away to the right. The Butte also becomes visible ahead, roughly in line with the track. Staying on this route, it soon reaches the Le Sars-Eaucourt road (D.11). **Cross the road** and r**ejoin the track**; from here onwards it is of much better quality. Before moving off, there is a good view to the Butte; the importance of its high position is clearly seen – it totally dominates the battlefield.

Continue on the track. Nearer the Butte it meets **another track** from

**View from the crest of the Butte towards Le Sars village.**

**the right. Join this** and **go left.** Just **before the main Albert-Bapaume road** (D.929) turn **sharp right** up a minor metalled road going uphill. This leads to the Butte de Warlencourt. The top of the Butte is reached by followed a well trodden path through the trees and undergrowth, and up a flight of **makeshift stairs with a handrail** to the top. In wet weather this route can be slippery, and signs warn visitors they are entering at their own risk.

The Butte de Warlencourt is an ancient burial mound, possibly of Gallo-Romano origin given that the Roman Albert-Bapaume road runs close by. It figured in the 1916 Somme fighting after the capture of High Wood, Martinpuich, and later, Le Sars. The Germans tunnelled through the mound, making deep dugouts and defensive positions. More importantly it was used as an observation post. From here a German Forward Observation Officer could see the approaching ground for some miles. With a field telephone or runners, he could then call down fire on any advancing forces in this area. In this respect the Butte dominated the whole battlefield here, and continued to do so throughout the latter stages of the Battle of the Somme.

There were a number of attacks on the Butte de Warlencourt, involving Scottish, South African and British troops. One of the more famous was in November 1916 when the 1/9th Durham Light Infantry advanced on the Butte. The 9th DLI were commanded by a highly

198

respected officer, Lieutenant-Colonel Roland Boys Bradford. Bradford, a pre-war territorial officer and still only twenty-four years old, had served in several battalions of the DLI in 1915 before coming to command the 9th. He had been awarded a Victoria Cross for bravery in leading his battalion at Eaucourt L'Abbaye in October. On 5th November Bradford was again leading his men into a difficult operation around the Butte. Bad weather had turned the ground into a muddy morass, and it was over such difficult terrain that 9th DLI attacked that day. They came up from south of the Butte, captured trenches around it and set up posts flanking the position. However, 'mopping up' parties had failed to clear all the German dugouts, and now the enemy brought fire to bear on Bradford's men. Heavy German counter-attacks followed, and slowly 9th DLI's garrison dwindled in numbers, ammunition and supplies. Later that night a very strong counter-attack by Bavarian troops pushed what men remained back to trenches away from the Butte. In some cases men had refused to retreat and fought to the last round. It was a sad battalion that paraded outside their bivouacs at Mametz Wood the next day; there had been over 400 casualties. Bradford himself had not been happy with the operation, and made the following reflections in a report he wrote soon afterwards:

**Roland Boys Bradford VC**

> 'On looking back at the attack of the 5th of November it seems that the results which would have been gained in the event of success were of doubtful value, and would hardly have been worth the loss which we would suffer. It would have been awkward for us to hold the objectives which would have been badly sited for defence. The Butte itself would have been of little use to us for the purposes of observation. But the Butte de Warlencourt had become an obsession. Everybody wanted it. It loomed large in the minds of the soldiers in the forward area and they attributed many of their misfortunes to it. The newspaper correspondents talked about 'that Miniature Gibralter'. So it had to be taken. It seems that the attack was one of those of tempting, and unfortunately at one period frequent, local operations which are so costly and which are rarely worthwhile. But perhaps that is only the narrow view of the Regimental Officer.'[2]

However, someone was listening to Bradford. He was a popular and highly respected officer among all ranks. No-one was surprised when, at the age of twenty-five, he was promoted acting Brigadier-General and sent to command a brigade in the 62nd (West Riding) Division at the Battle of Cambrai in November 1917. On 30th November, just over a year since he had been battling with his old battalion on the Butte de

199

Warlencourt, Bradford's luck finally ran out. A shell struck his brigade headquarters, and Roland Boys Bradford VC MC – the so-called 'Boy General' – was mortally wounded; he died of these wounds in the crypt of Hermies church. Today his grave can be found in Hermies British Cemetery (F-10).

The Butte de Warlencourt was never taken during the 1916 Battle of the Somme; local fighting came to an end here on 18th November when a snowstorm signalled the end of the Somme. Throughout that Winter the Germans were able to look down on the British lines in the valley before the Butte, making life in the front line very difficult, aside from the poor weather. It finally passed into British hands when the Germans withdrew from the area in the Spring of 1917, during the Retreat to the Hindenburg Line. A number of wooden crosses were erected at that time- one of them commemorating Bradford's 9th DLI. Today this cross in is Durham cathedral. The Butte de Warlencourt is now owned by the Western Front Association, a Great War remembrance organisation founded by author John Giles in 1980. It was his idea that the Association should acquire and preserve the Butte. New memorials have been erected on the summit, and much of the undergrowth cleared away so that the views afforded to the Germans in 1916 can be fully appreciated. An orientation table originally planned to be sited on the Butte can now be seen in the Musee des Abris in Albert.

**Western Front Association memorial on the Butte de Warlencourt.**

Leaving the Butte return via the metalled minor road downhill. At the bottom it meets the track you came up from the left. **Turn right** onto the main Albert-Road, and on the main road turn left in the direction of Le Sars – visible ahead up the hill. This is a busy road and it is sensible to walk on the grass verge. **Stay on this verge** until the outskirts of the village are reached. A civilian cemetery is on the left; there are good views from here back towards the Butte showing how the British saw the ground. On the left just past the cemetery and a large brown brick-built crypt, the entrance to a track appears. Follow this as it curves round the back of the village. Le Sars was finally captured by units of the 23rd Division on 7th October 1916, after they had made several attempts in the preceding week. The village itself was cleared by a mixed party of 9th Yorkshires and 13th Durhams, who met at the cross-roads in the village. By this time Le Sars had been reduced to rubble. **Stay on the track** as it passes back gardens and allotments until it meets the Le Sars-Eaucourt road (D.11); **at this junction cross the road** and rejoin the **track opposite**.

As the western outskirts of the village are reached by this track, a junction of tracks is encountered. Before proceeding there are some farm buildings on the right – between the track you are on and the farm is a large grey stone. This is an original 1916 memorial to the German 111th Reserve Infantry Regiment. Constructed when Le Sars was some way behind the front line it was part of a large German cemetery that was destroyed in later fighting. It commemorates 'fallen comrades' of 111th RIR and lists the battle honours of 'Fricourt, Mametz,

**Le Sars mid 1916.**

Montauban and La Boisselle'. Indeed, this unit was holding the line east of Fricourt on 1st July 1916. Although showing signs of original shell damage, the memorial is otherwise in good condition. At the junction of the tracks, go left following a track back in the direction of Martinpuich. Further along the track there are good views on the right towards Pozières Windmill and Courcelette; this ground was fought over between September and November 1916. Later the track becomes sunken, and beyond this it meets the main D.6E Martinpuich road. **Turn left** onto this road. A little further along, before the road begins to slope downwards, stop and look to the left; there is a good panoramic view across the ground you have covered on this walk.

Follow the road downhill and back into the outskirts of Martinpuich. Go through the village and back to the church and your vehicle.

## READING LIST

Anon.   *The Somme and the Butte de Warlencourt* (Western Front Association 1990)

Gladden, N. *The Somme 1916* (Kimber 1974)

# GUILLEMONT ROAD

STARTING POINT: **Car park, Delville Wood visitors' centre**
DURATION: **2 hours**
WALK SUMMARY: **A largely cross-country walk ideal for a novice walker. It covers the ground between Trones Wood and Guillemont where much fighting took place between July and September 1916. It makes good a good companion to the Dawn Attack Walk**.

*There are good parking facilities at Delville Wood, which are clearly signposted. The visitors' centre also boasts picnic facilities, a shop, tea room and good toilets.*

Leaving the car park **turn right** on the road back into Longueval and follow until a junction is reached by the local civilian cemetery on your left. At this **junction turn right**, again towards Longueval and stay on this road (D.20) for about two hundred yards until a **minor road** is seen **on the left. Take this** minor road which passes a few houses until fields on the outskirts of Longueval are reached. There are good views from here across the battlefield south of Longueval. Ahead is the large dark mass of Trones Wood, to the right of that the smaller Bernafay Wood, and Montauban is seen on the horizon to the far right. This area was advanced over on 14th July 1916; further details of this action can be found in the Dawn Attack Walk chapter.

Continue along this track, the surface of which was vastly improved in 1996 and is now metalled. Further along it is sunken, and then levels out again. Soon the northern tip of Trones Wood is reached, with trees appearing on the right. Trones Wood proved a great obstacle in the British advance after the successful attack on the Montauban-Mametz line on 1st July. The neighbouring Bernafay Wood to the west fell on 3rd July, and thereafter attacks were made on Trones Wood by units of the 18th (Eastern) Division which had done so well in the 1st July fighting. These attacks proved costly, and with little success until the Dawn Attack of 14th July when several battalions – among them 7th Royal West Kents, 6th Northamptonshires and 8th Royal Sussex Regiment (Pioneers) – finally captured the wood. The fighting was especially severe; one officer of the 7th Royal West Kents recalled that the Germans allowed his men to advance to within ten or twelve yards of their positions before opening fire and showering them with bombs at close range. The battalion lost 13 officers and 216 other ranks in this fighting. By a quirk of fate, the 18th Division returned to Trones Wood in August 1918 when the units who had taken the wood in 1916 were once again called on to retake it; one wonders how many men survived long enough to fight in both engagements?

**Continue along the track**. Further up there are good views towards Guillemont, and in the far distance on the left, Ginchy. Many divisions fought over this ground between July and September 1916; among them the Guards and the 16th (Irish) Division. Further down the track there is a small copse on the left. Go past this copse and the open ground before Guillemont is visible again. **Stop** and look towards the spire of

**Original wooden cross memorial to the 18th (Eastern) Division at Trones Wood, 1919.**

Guillemont church. It was over this ground that the 55th (West Lancs) Division made a number of attacks after the capture of Trones Wood on 14th July. This was a territorial division whose motto was 'They Win or Die, Who Wear The Rose of Lancaster', and was dominated by battalions of the King's Liverpool Regiment. One of these was the kilted Liverpool Scottish; the 1/10th King's Liverpool Regiment recruited from Scottish families in the Liverpool area. They made an attack on Guillemont on 9th August when four separate advances were beaten back with heavy losses.

One of those responsible for attending to the wounded on that day was the medical officer of the Liverpool Scottish – Captain Noel Gordon Chavasse MC. Educated at Liverpool and Oxford, where he excelled as an athlete with his twin brother Christopher, Noel Chavasse trained as a doctor and practised in Liverpool from 1912. He joined the Liverpool Scottish as their MO in 1913, and served with them in France from November 1914. For bravery at Hooge in 1915 he had been awarded the Military Cross. Here at Guillemont he:

**Noel Gordon Chavasse VC**

'... continued to tend the wounded in the open all day under a heavy fire, frequently exposing himself to view of the enemy. He organised parties to get the wounded away most successfully. That night he spent four hours searching the ground in front of the enemy's lines for wounded lying out. On the following day... he carried an urgent case for 500 yards to safety under a very heavy shell fire. During this performance he was wounded in the side by a shell splinter. The same night he took a party of 20 volunteers, and succeeded in recovering three more of the wounded from a shell hole 25 yards from the German trench, buried the bodies of two officers, and collected a number of identity discs, although fired on by bombs and machine-guns. Altogether this officer was the means of saving the lives of 20 seriously wounded men under the most trying circumstances, besides the ordinary cases which passed through his hands. At one time, when all the officers were shot down, he helped to rally the firing line.'[1]

For these gallant acts, Noel Gordon Chavasse was awarded the Victoria Cross. This exceptionally brave officer went on to serve in the Ypres

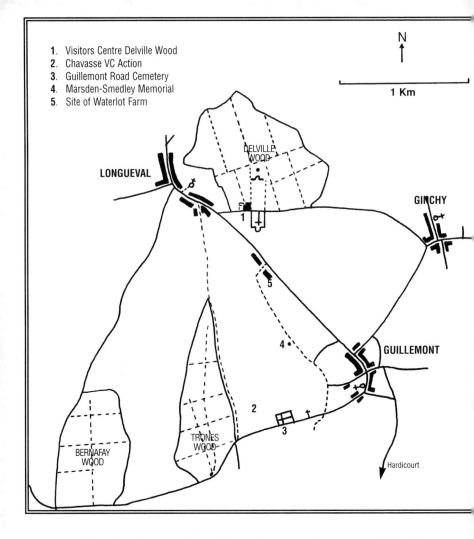

1. Visitors Centre Delville Wood
2. Chavasse VC Action
3. Guillemont Road Cemetery
4. Marsden-Smedley Memorial
5. Site of Waterlot Farm

N

1 Km

LONGUEVAL

DELVILLE WOOD

GINCHY

GUILLEMONT

TRONES WOOD

BERNAFAY WOOD

Hardicourt

Salient; for further gallantry in rescuing wounded in front of Wieltje on 31st July 1917, he received a bar to his Victoria Cross – only the second man to do so in the history of the VC, and the only one to receive both awards during the Great War. Sadly, it was to be a posthumous award; Noel Chavasse was badly wounded in the head at Wieltje and died of these wounds in a Casualty Clearing Station at Brandhoek. Today his final resting place can be found in Brandhoek New Military Cemetery; a unique gravestone which has the emblems of two Victoria Crosses on it.

Again continue along the metalled track until is meets the main road (D.64) at the southern edge of Trones Wood. A minor diversion to visit the 18th Division memorial can be made here by **turning right**; the

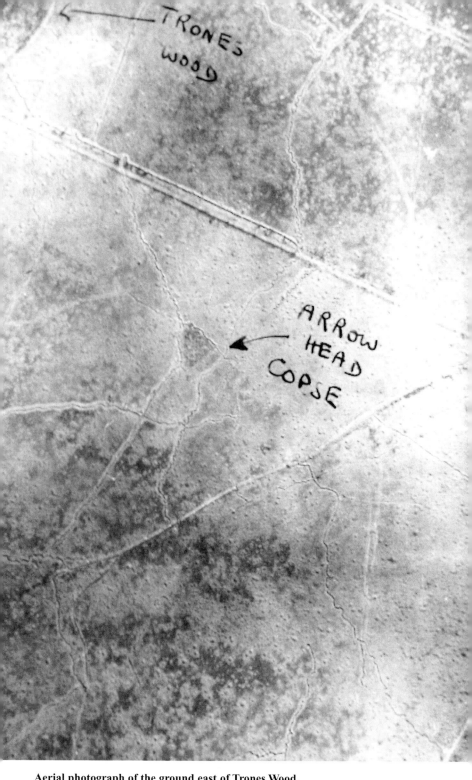

**Aerial photograph of the ground east of Trones Wood.**

memorial is on the edge of the wood by the road after a short walk of about two hundred yards. It commemorates their successful capture of the wood in both 1916 and 1918. After visiting, **retrace your steps** and continue on the D.64 to the military cemetery. **Otherwise turn left** at the junction of track and road, and follow the D.64 to Guillemont Road Cemetery.

## GUILLEMONT ROAD CEMETERY

The burials were begun by the Field Ambulances in the Guards Division during the fighting for Guillemont in September 1916; the cemetery remained in use until March 1917 by which time there were 121 graves. These now form Plot I of the current cemetery. After the war some 2,139 graves were brought in from the Guillemont-Ginchy battlefield enlarging Guillemont Road Cemetery to 2,251 British burials along with one each from Canada, Australia, South Africa and Newfoundland.

Perhaps the most visited grave in the cemetery is that of Lieutenant Raymond Asquith (I-B-3), son of the then Prime Minister, H.H. Asquith. Considered a man of great promise by all who knew him, his early death on the Somme was seen as a great tragedy by some of the leading political and social figures of the day. Asquith had joined the

**Guillemont Road Cemetery 1919.**

Edition Vve Bauchart — Cliché Lelong à St-Fuscien

3rd Grenadier Guards in 1915, and was killed in the Guards' attack on Guillemont on 15th September 1916. The original cross that once stood on this grave was acquired by the Asquith family after the war and can be seen in the church at Mells in Somerset, where the Asquiths had their home. A few graves away from Raymond Asquith is the grave of his friend, and relation by marriage, Lieutenant Edward Wyndham Tennant (I-B-18). Known as 'BIM' to his friends, he was killed a week after Asquith with the 4th Grenadier Guards on 22nd September 1916, aged nineteen. An aspiring young poet, his work showed great promise; two of his finest pieces are 'Homes Thoughts in Laventie' and 'The Mad Soldier'.

Another interesting officer, buried in an isolated grave close to the cemetery entrance, is Second Lieutenant W.A. Stanhope Forbes (I-A-1). Killed with the Duke of Cornwall's Light Infantry on 3rd September 1916, aged twenty-three, he was the son of the painter Stanhope Forbes R.A. His father chose a fine inscription for the headstone, which reads, 'He saw beyond the filth of battle and thought death a fair price to pay to belong to the company of these fellows'. In Plot I there are a large number of Royal Army Medical Corps graves; showing how various Field Ambulances close to the line buried their own dead as well as the wounded and dying who passed through their hands. In particular are two large burials from the 4th and 19th Field Ambulances, with another grouping from the 101st Field Ambulance.

Leaving the cemetery **turn left** onto the D.64 in the direction of Guillemont. A small calvary is soon passed on the left. Further up **on the left** a track opens up – follow this. The track winds on for a couple of hundred yards where it meets another coming in from Guillemont village. This track, like others in the area, was metalled in 1996. Follow the track to the left, past wired off fields and the remains of Guillemont quarry on the right, going roughly north back in the direction of Longueval. This area was heavily fought over in August and September 1916, and German author Ernst Junger was here with the 73rd Hannovarians at that time. His experiences are related in *Storm of Steel*. The metalled track continues, with views to Trones Wood on the left, and Guillemont on the right; Longueval and Delville Wood are ahead. Soon the track comes in line with a huge grain silo on the right; on the left in a field just off the track is a small, walled memorial.

## MARSDEN-SMEDLEY MEMORIAL

George Futvoye Marsden-Smedley was a young Rifle Brigade officer killed near Guillemont on 18th August 1916, aged nineteen. Born at Matlock, Derbyshire, and educated at Harrow, Marsden-

**Marsden-Smedley Memorial with Trones Wood in the background.**

**Waterlot Farm 1914.**

Smedley had only joined the 3rd Battalion Rifle Brigade a month or so before his death. His body was never found, and after the war his parents purchased this plot of land, near to where he was last seen alive. The current memorial was erected by them in the early 1920s. In recent years it fell into disrepair, but members of the Marsden-Smedley family and the Western Front Association are currently in the process of restoring it. George Marsden-Smedley's name can also be found on the Thiepval Memorial.

Return to the track, and continue in the direction of Longueval. A little past the Marsden-Smedley memorial the track loses its metalled surface and runs alongside a large embankment on the right. Signs of dugouts and guns positions from later fighting are visible here. Stay on the track until the embankment ends; then **turn right**, past the ruins of Waterlot Farm. Waterlot Farm was the name given by the British to the ruins of a sugar refinery just off the Longueval-Guillemont road. It was a large complex, heavily fortified by the Germans. Finally captured in late July 1916, the 17th (Football) Battalion Middlesex Regiment made a costly attack near here in early August. It was rebuilt after the war, and again used as a sugar refinery. the somewhat ugly buildings were disused by the late 1960s, until demolished in 1993.

**Follow the track** from the ruins of Waterlot Farm between some houses until it reaches the main Guillemont-Longueval road (D.20). **Turn left** in the direction of Longueval, past a row of houses on the left.

**Men resting in a shell hole near Waterlot Farm.**

**The Guillemont Road, September 1916.**  *John Giles*

The road eventually reaches the junction by Longueval civilian
cemetery; **turn right** here and follow the signs back to Delville Wood
car park and your vehicle.

## READING LIST

Clayton, A.   *Chavasse Double VC* (Pen & Sword 1992)
Jolliffe, J.   *Raymond Asquith: Life and Letters* (Collins 1980)
Junger, E.   *Storm of Steel* (Chatto & Windus 1929)
Powell, A.   *'BIM'- A Tribute to The Honourable Edward Wyndham
                Tennant 1897-1916* (Anne Powell 1990)

# ABBREVIATIONS

| | |
|---|---|
| Pte | Private |
| Pnr | Pioneer |
| Dmr | Drummer |
| A/Bmdr | Acting Bombardier |
| L/Cpl | Lance Corporal |
| Cpl | Corporal |
| L/Sgt | Lance Sergeant |
| Sgt | Sergeant |
| CSM | Company Sergeant Major |
| CQMS | Company Quarter Master Sergeant |
| RSM | Regimental Sergeant Major |
| 2/Lt | Second Lieutenant |
| Lieut | Lieutenant |
| Capt | Captain |
| Lt-Col | Lieutenant-Colonel |
| Col | Colonel |
| Brig-Gen | Brigadier-General |
| Lt-Gen | Lieutenant-General |
| O.C. | Officer Commanding |
| CRA | Commander Royal Artillery |
| AIF | Australian Imperial Force |
| ADS | Advanced Dressing Station |
| ASC | Army Service Corps |
| Bn | Battalion |
| Bty | Battery |
| KOYLI | King's Own Yorkshire Light Infantry |
| KRRC | King's Royal Rifle Corps |
| NZEF | New Zealand Expeditionary Force |
| RAMC | Royal Army Medical Corps |
| RAP | Regimental Aid Post |
| RE | Royal Engineers |
| RFA | Royal Field Artillery |
| RFC | Royal Flying Corps |
| RGA | Royal Garrison Artillery |
| RHA | Royal Horse Artillery |
| RND | Royal Naval Division |
| RWF | Royal Welsh Fusiliers |
| VC | Victoria Cross |
| DSO | Distinguished Service Order |

| | |
|---|---|
| MC | Military Cross |
| DCM | Distinguished Conduct Medal |
| MM | Military Medal |
| CWGC | Commonwealth War Graves Commission |

## GRAVE LOCATION IN CEMETERIES

| | |
|---|---|
| (B-22) | Row B : Grave 22 |
| (I-C-17) | Plot 1 : Row C : Grave 17 |

# ENDNOTES

**PREFACE**
(1) Douie, C. *The Weary Road* (Murray 1929).

**GOMMECOURT WALK**
(1) Interview with author, 1983.
(2) ibid.
(3) Dudley-Ward, C.H. *The 56th Division* (John Murray 1931).
(4) Quoted from '46th North Midland Division TF Court of Inquiry into Operations at Gommecourt 1st July 1916' PRO WO95/2663.
(5) *London Gazette* 4.8.16.

**THE PALS WALK- SERRE**
(1) Blunden, E. *Undertones of War* (Cobden Sanderson 1928).
(2) Quoted from private papers in the author's archives.
(3) War Diary 13th Bn East Yorkshire Regiment 13.11.16 PRO WO95/2357.
(4) *London Gazette* 13.1.17.
(5) War Diary 13th Bn East Yorkshire Regiment op cit.

**BEAUMONT-HAMEL WALK**
(1) From an interview with the author, 1983.
(2) From papers in the author's archives.
(3) Quoted from 'Account of the 1st July battle by 86 Brigade' in War Diary 29th Division Headquarters 7.7.16 PRO WO95/2300.
(4) From papers in the author's archives.
(5) Malins, G. *How I Filmed The War* (Herbert Jenkins 1920).

**ANCRE VALLEY WALK**
(1) War Diary 1st Newfoundland Regiment 1.7.16 PRO WO95/2308.
(2) Williamson, Henry *Love and the Loveless* (Macdonald 1958) is one novel in a fifteen novel sequence entitled 'A Chronicle of Ancient Sunlight'. No knowledge of the Great War is complete without reference to these fine books which are currently (1996) being reprinted by Alan Sutton.
(3) From papers in the author's archives.
(4) From an account in the author's archives.
(5) *London Gazette* 15.12.16.

**THIEPVAL WALK**
(1) Douie, C. *The Weary Road* (Murray 1929).
(2) ibid.
(3) Coppard, G. *With A Machine-gun to Cambrai* (1969).
(4) *London Gazette* 25.9.16.

**THE AIF WALK- POZIERES**
(1) Edmonds, C. *A Subaltern's War* (Peter Davies 1929).
(2) *London Gazette* 9.9.16.
(3) Bean, C.E.W. *AIF In France* Vol III 1916 (Sydney 1923).
(4) Bean op cit.
(5) ibid.
(6) ibid.
(7) His grave can be found in Puchevillers British Cemetery (III-A-6).
(8) *London Gazette* 26.9.16.
(9) Bean op cit.

**THE YORKSHIRE WALK- FRICOURT**
(1) Spicer, L.D. *Letters From France 1915-18* (Robert York 1979).
(2) *London Gazette* 8.9.16.
(3) He has no known grave and is commemorated on the Soissons Memorial.

**THE POET'S WALK**
(1) Adams, B. *Nothing Of Importance* (Methuen 1917).
(2) ibid.

(3)  Hart-Davies, R. (Ed) *Siegfried Sassoon Diaries 1915-1918* (Faber and Faber 1983).
(4)  Adams op cit.
(5)  *London Gazette* June 1916.
(6)  Hodgson, W.N. *Verse and Prose in Peace and War* (Smith, Elder & Co 1916).
(7)  Plowman, M. *A Subaltern on the Somme in 1916* (Dent 1927).

**BEHIND THE LINES WALK**
(1)  Blunden, E.  *Undertones of War* (Cobden Sanderson 1928).

**MONTAUBAN WALK**
(1)  Grant, D.F. *History of 'A' Battery 84th Brigade R.F.A.* (Marshall Brothers 1922).
(2)  ibid.
(3)  From correspondence with the author, 1986.

**THE DAWN ATTACK WALK**
(1)  9th Division Headquarters papers PRO WO95/1735.
(2)  Quoted in translation from the German Official History *Bilder aus der Sommeschlact*.
(3)  Quoted from 'The Story of Delville Wood: Told in letters from the Front'(no date, no publisher, c.1916).
(4)  *London Gazette* 26.10.16.

**BUTTE DE WARLENCOURT WALK**
(1)  Maude, A.H. (Ed) *The 47th (London) Division 1914-1919* (Amalgamated Press1922).
(2)  Quoted in Anon. *The Somme and the Butte de Warlencourt* (Western Front Association 1990).

**GUILLEMONT ROAD WALK**
(1)  *London Gazette* 26.10.16.

# ACKNOWLEDGEMENTS

First, Bill Hogg deserves his own mention. Bill is one of the few pioneers in walking the battlefields, and willingly gave his time, experience and much other help when I first began visiting the Western Front in the early 1980s.

Thanks to all those who have walked the Somme with me during the research for this book: among them – Stephen Clarke, John Dray, Colin Fox, Ali Herd, Maurice Johnson, Tony & Joan Poucher, Terry Russell, Vic Sayer, Tony Spagnoly, Frank and Lou Stockdale, Ken Turner, Pam Waugh, and Michelle and Wayne Young. In France thanks goes to: Steve Austin, Madame Josiane Brihier, Bernard Delsert, Elise Dolivet, Michel Duthoit of Hotel de la Paix, Tom and Janet Fairgrieve, and Bernard Leguillier. Roy Evans of Cheadle was good enough to share his knowledge of the 62nd Division with me, and gave useful information on Val Braithwaite's father.

I was fortunate enough to interview many veterans over the years, several of whom became family friends. In particular I would like to mention: Albert Banfield, George Butler, Harry Coates, Horace Hamm, Leslie Lovegrove, Frank Plumb, Aubrey Rose, and Malcolm Vyvyan MC. Sadly, like all old soldiers, they have faded away with time and age- but I shall never forgot them, or their like, and consider my life to have been all the richer for having known them.

For more years than I care to remember Yves and Christian Foucat of Pozieres have shown myself and many friends great hospitality and kindness, and were always willing to share their unique knowledge of the Somme and their superb collection of battlefield artefacts they have built up over more than a quarter of a century. Since having a house on the Somme, Yves and Christian have helped Kieron and I in more ways than we could ever repay, and for that we are especially grateful. Those who know them will agree France and the French people could not have two greater ambassadors. A mention must also be made of the 'Sussex Pals' with whom I visited the battlefields for many years: Geoff Bridger, Brian Fullagar, Geoff Goodyear, Clive Metcalfe, Colin Roberts, Julian Sykes, Terry Whippy, and Andrew Whittington.

John and Margery Giles, to whom the book is dedicated, proved to be good friends over the many years I knew John, and continue to know Margery. John has his own monument in the shape of his books which inspire new generations of battlefield visitors.

A special thank you must also go to my parents, who have always encouraged and supported my frequently obsessive interest in the Great War. My mother in particular has seemingly spent many of her holidays turning up rare unit histories in the most obscure of book shops!

The staff of the Public Record Office at Kew have always been helpful, and the Commonwealth War Graves Commission willingly searched their records on my behalf many times. Great War historian Norm Christie, formerly of their Maidenhead and Beaurains offices, now working as a free-lance researcher in Canada, was most helpful in answering enquiries about the original burial place of James Crozier.

The author and publishers wish to thank the following for permission to reproduce extracts from material for which they hold the copyright: Faber & Faber for *Siegfried Sassoon Diaries 1915-18*, John Murray Ltd for *The 56th Division* and *The Weary Road*. Every effort has been made to trace the owners of quoted material, and the author and publishers apologise for any omissions.

All photographs are from the author's archives unless otherwise credited. I am particularly grateful to Klaus Spath of Backnang, Germany, who allowed me access to his extensive collection of German photographs.

Last, and by no means least, my love and thanks go to Kieron, who not only walked much of the ground covered in the book but offered constructive ideas and helped with many endless tasks. To her, I say, as ever... 'toujours'.

# SELECTIVE INDEX

Accrington 38, 39, 40

Adams, Bernard 127-129

Albert 86, 89, 160

Allenby, Gen. 17

Ancre River 79-80, 83, 86, 88, 101

Asquith, Raymond 208-209

Auchonvillers 36, 45, 46-8, 49, 53, 65, 66, 81, 149-152, 160, 161, 162

**Australian Imperial Force (AIF)**
    **Divisions:1**(Aust) 105, 106, 107, 112
    **Brigades: 1**(Aust) 107
    **3**(Aust) 105
    **Battalions and Corps: 4** Bn 106
    **7** Bn 106
    **8** Bn 106, 107, 114
    **14** Bn 108
    **18** Bn 114
    **22** Bn 114
    **27** Bn 110
    **48** Bn 108-109
    **11** Bde AFA 191
    **5** Coy AMGC 114
    **7** Coy AMGC 110

Authuille 83, 86, 102

Aveluy 86, 87, 89

Aveluy Wood 83, 160

Ayre Family 70-71, 75, 161


Bazentin-le-Grand 173, 177

Bazentin-le-Petit 166, 173, 174-179, 181, 183

Bean, Charles 107, 114

Beaucourt 74, 75, 76, 77, 78-79, 160

Beaumont-Hamel 67-75, 149

Becourt 116, 118, 140

Becourt Wood 118

Bienvillers-au-Bois 24

Blunden, Edmund 34, 46, 49, 77, 149-150, 158

Bois Francais 121, 127-133

Boom Ravine 15

Boote, C.E. Lt-Col 24

Braithwaite, Val Lt 35

**British Army**
    **Armies:**
        **Third Army** 17, 115
        **Fifth Army** 115
    **Corps:**
        **V Corps** 32, 59, 75
        **VII Corps** 17
        **XIII Corps** 166
        **XV Corps** 166

    **Divisions:**
        **1** Guards 184
        **3** 42, 163, 167, 168, 173
        **4** 29-30, 31, 37, 61, 63, 149, 151, 154, 161
        **7** 127, 129, 130, 174
        **8** 83, 89

    **9** 163, 167, 168, 169
    **12** 86, 154
    **14** 184, 187
    **15** 194
    **16** 94, 176, 204
    **17** 118
    **18** 96,102, 130,139,142,144,145, 164, 203-204, 206
    **21** 118, 121
    **23** 201
    **24** 129
    **29** 46, 49, 53, 60, 63, 67, 71, 155, 160
    **30** 139, 145, 147, 164
    **31** 31, 37, 42, 43
    **32** 83, 157
    **36** 75, 77, 80, 81, 83, 97, 100, 151, 161
    **38** 87
    **39** 80, 160
    **41** 188-192
    **42** 27
    **46** 19, 22-24, 26-27
    **47** 180, 194, 197
    **48** 13, 15, 31, 103, 105, 112, 114
    **49** 83, 97
    **50** 175
    **51** 61, 63, 71-73, 75, 83, 155
    **55** 184, 205
    **56** 15-17, 20-23, 27
    **62** 35, 199
    **63** (RND) 71, 75, 77-78, 93, 158, 160
    **NZ 29**, 151, 182
**Brigades:**
    **1** Guards 186
    **8** 173
    **9** 173
    **11** 35
    **26** 167, 168
    **27** 167, 168
    **42** 187
    **55** 143
    **63** 118
    **64** 118
    **70** 87
    **86** 53
    **92** 42
    **122** 188, 190
    **137** 22
    **139** 22
    **140** 197
    **141** 197
    **145** 105
    **168** 20, 21
    **169** 17, 19-20, 21 27
**Battalions:**
    1/7 Argylls 154
    1/8 Argylls 62
    4/Bedfords 161

7/Bedfords 100
4/5 Black Watch 80
1/Borders 162
11/Borders 90, 92
1/1 Bucks Bn 105
1/Camerons 181
1/6 Cheshires 80
1/Coldstream Gds 129
2/Coldstream Gds 186
3/Coldstream Gds 186-187
6/Connaught Rangers 141
8/Devons 133, 134-135
9/Devons 133, 134-135
1/Dorsets 83, 85, 91, 92, 192
1/9 DLI 198-200
10/DLI 193
13/DLI 95, 201
1/East Lancs 61
11/East Lancs 38, 40
8/East Surreys 141, 143
7/East Yorks 116, 121, 122
8/East Yorks 173
10/East Yorks 42-43
11/East Yorks 42-43, 161
12/East Yorks 42-43
13/East Yorks 42-43, 161
1/Essex 68, 70
2/Essex 37
1/6 Gloucesters 105
10/Gloucesters 176
2/Grenadier Gds 129
3/Grenadier Gds 209
4/Grenadier Gds 209
1/Hampshires 30, 63-64
Hawke Bn RND 76
1/9 HLI 180
17/HLI 91, 92
Hood Bn RND 78
10/Inniskilling Fus 97
1/10 Kings Liverpools 205
1/Kings Own 37
2/KOSB 39
2/KOYLI 140, 158
5/KOYLI 85
6/KOYLI 184
8/KOYLI 87, 89
9/KOYLI 116, 117, 118-119
1/KRRC 172
21/KRRC 191-192
1/Lanc Fus 53, 62, 63-64
15/Lanc Fus 91, 96, 102
1/4 Lincolns 27
8/Lincolns 21
Liverpool Pals 146-148, 182
London Regiment 15, 27, 93,
179, 197
1/3 Londons 27
12/Londons 19-20, 22
London Rifle Brigade 17-19, 22
London Scottish 15
8/Loyal North Lancs 91
10/Loyal North Lancs 176
2/Manchesters 90

4/Middlesex 120
16/Middlesex 50, 53, 54, 57, 60,
63, 151
17/Middlesex 211
2/Monmouths 60
1/Newfoundland Regt 67-72, 75,
154, 160, 161
8/Norfolks 71
1/5 North Staffs 24
1/Northants 175-176
6/Northants 203
1/Northumberland Fus 173
16/Northumberland Fus 102
1/4 Oxfs & Bucks L.I. 15, 105
Queen Victoria's Rifles 19, 21, 22
Queens Westminster Rifles 19-20
1/Rifle Brigade 161
2/Rifle Brigade 89
3/Rifle Brigade 211
1/4 Royal Berks 105
1/Royal Dublin Fus 53, 151
9/Royal Dublin Fus 94
2/Royal Fus 53-57, 94
10/Royal Fus 25
20/Royal Fus 180
22/Royal Fus 37, 95
6/Royal Irish Rif 141
8/Royal Irish Rif 97
9/Royal Irish Rif 31, 81, 85,
100,157
14/Royal Irish Rif 97
15/Royal Irish Rif 101
12/Royal Scots 141
2/Royal Sussex 172-173, 182
8/Royal Sussex 203
11/Royal Sussex 35, 46, 49, 77,
150, 158
1/Royal Welsh Fus 127-130, 131
2/Royal Welsh Fus 175, 177
16/Royal Welsh Fus 141
1/Royal West Kents 182
7/Royal West Kents 143,
145, 203
11/Royal West Kents 188, 190
2/Seaforths 31, 154
1/5 Seaforths 61
9/Scottish Rifles 167-168
1/5 Sherwood Foresters 23, 26
1/7 Sherwood Foresters 23
11/Sherwood Foresters 87, 89
16/Sherwood Foresters 80
1/Somerset Light Inf 30,
35-36, 160
8/South Lancs 97
1/6 South Staffs 24
8/South Staffs 124
2/SWB 71
1/6 West Yorks 101
10/West Yorks 116, 121, 122
15/West Yorks 38, 40
16/West Yorks 38, 94
10/Worcesters 178
2/York & Lancs 158

8/York & Lancs 87, 89
9/York & Lancs 87, 89
12/York & Lancs 35, 39, 40, 41
6/Yorkshires 87
7/Yorkshires 116, 124, 125
9/Yorkshires 201
10/Yorkshires 116, 117, 119-120

**Corps:**

Heavy Branch MGC 163
A Bn Heavy Branch MGC 100
37 Coy MGC 88
86 Coy MGC 62
208 Coy MGC 75
Royal Army Medical Corps 49, 75, 127, 140, 163, 209
12th Field Amb RAMC 151
Royal Engineers 86, 131, 168
178 Tunneling Coy RE 116, 181
252 Tunneling Coy RE 54, 62, 151, 154
Royal Field Artillery 163
A/84 Bde RFA 143-145
B Bty RHA 60
86 Trench Mortar Bty 62, 63

Bromilow, J.N. Mjr 37
Brooke, Rupert 78
Bull, A.E. Pte 35, 39
Butte de Warlencourt 182, 194-202
Butterworth, G.S.K. Lt 95

Carnoy 133, 139-142
Carnoy Craters 144-145
Carrington, Charles 105-106
Cemeteries, British
  AIF Burial Ground 191-192
  Auchonvillers Comm Cem 162
  Auchonvillers Mil Cem 151-152
  Authuille Mil Cem 83-85, 102
  Bazentin-le-Petit Comm Cem 174, 183
  Bazentin-le-Petit Comm Cem Ext 175-176
  Beaumont-Hamel Brit Cem 62-63
  Blighty Valley Cem 86, 87, 89
  Bulls Road Cem 189-191
  Carnoy Mil Cem 71, 139-141, 148
  Citadel New Mil Cem 127-129, 138
  Connaught Cem 97-100
  Couin Mil Cem 129
  Delville Wood Cem 171-173
  Devonshire Cem 133-134
  Englebelmer Comm Cem 158
  Englebelmer Comm Cem Ext 158, 160
  Foncquevillers Mil Cem 5-27
  Fricourt New Mil Cem 122
  Fricourt (Bray Road) Cem 124-125, 137
  Gommecourt No 2 Brit Cem 15, 20-21
  Gommecourt Wood New Cem 23-24
  Guillemont Road Cem 208-209
  Hawthorn Ridge No 1 Cem 50, 59-61
  Hawthorn Ridge No 2 Cem 72
  Hebuterne Mil Cem 13-15, 23
  Hunters Cem 71, 72
  Knightsbridge Cem 71, 160-161
  Lonsdale Cem 90-91

Louvencourt Mil Cem 36, 66, 160
Luke Copse Cem 41
Mailly Comm Cem Ext 153-154
Mailly Wood Cem 154-156
Mesnil Ridge Cem 161
Mill Road Cem 97, 100
Norfolk Cem 116-118, 120, 126
Point 110 New Cem 129-131
Point 110 Old Cem 130-131
Pozieres Brit Cem 106, 113-115
Quarry Cem 163, 167, 173
Queens Cem 40-41
Railway Hollow Cem 40, 45
Redan Ridge Cem No 2 63-64
Serre Road No 1 Cem 37
Serre Road No 2 Cem 31, 32-35, 45
Serre Road No 3 Cem 38, 45
Sucrerie Cem 29-31, 45, 157
Thiepval Anglo-French Cem 95
Thistle Dump Cem 182-183
Y Ravine Cem 71
Cemeteries, French
  Serre National Cem 36-37
Chorley Company 39
Churchill, Winston 76, 77
Citadel Camp 127, 129
Courcelette 104, 107, 110, 111, 171, 202
Crozier, F.P. Lt-Col 157
Crozier, James 31, 157
Crucifix Corner (Aveluy) 88
Crucifix Corner (Bazentin) 177, 183

Delville Wood 166, 168, 169-172, 184, 187, 192-193, 203, 212
Destrube brothers 37
Douie, Charles 83, 85, 91

Eaucourt L'Abbaye 182, 195-197
Eden, Anthony 192
Englebelmer 149, 157-160

Feversham, Earl 191-192
Flers 187-192
Foncquevillers 23, 24-27
Forceville 66
French Army 36-37, 132, 162, 186, 192
Fricourt 116-126, 137-138
Fricourt Wood 121, 125, 137

**German Regiments**

14 Bavarian 187
16 Bavarian 168
66 RIR 42
111 RIR 201
119 RIR 56, 74
Gibralter Pillbox 104, 106, 112-113
Giles, R. Pte 94
Ginchy 94, 129, 169, 184, 186, 187, 204
Graves, Robert 127, 130, 131, 175
Guillemont 129, 169, 204-205, 209
Guyon, G.S. Mjr 93-94

Haig, Sir Douglas 164, 166
Hamel 46, 67, 80, 81, 100, 158, 160
Harmsworth, Vere 75-76
Harris, John 38

Hawthorn Mine Crater 31, 61, 66
Hawthorn Ridge 31, 49-66, 72, 74, 79, 151, 153, 154, 157, 161
Heaton, Eric 2/Lt 50, 57-60
Hebuterne 13-15, 31, 44
Heidenkopf 30, 31, 32, 35-36
High Wood 72, 94, 172-173, 174-183, 194, 198
Hodgson, William Noel 127, 134-135
Hull 42-43, 161

John Copse 38
Junger, Ernst 21

Kaiser's Oak 27
Kettle, Tom 94-95
Kipling, Rudyard 95

La Boisselle 118, 121
La Signy Farm 31, 40, 44-45
Le Sars 182, 197, 198, 200-202
Leipzig Redoubt 90, 91, 92, 101-102
Lochnagar Crater 118, 121
Longueval 166, 167, 168-169, 173, 181, 182, 193, 203, 211-212
Luke Copse 38, 41, 43
Lutyens, Sir Edwin 93
Lynch, C.W.D. Lt-Col 116-117, 118-119

Mailly-Maillet 29, 31, 46, 65, 66, 149, 152, 156-157
Mametz 134-137
Manning, Frederick 173
Mansel Copse 133-137
Mark Copse 31, 38, 45
Martin, D.L. Capt 133-134
Martinpuich 155, 175, 176, 177, 179, 181, 194-195, 198, 202
Matthew Copse 38, 45
Memorials, British
  1st Australian Division 112
  20th Royal Fusiliers 180
  47th (London) Division 180-181
  51st (Highland) Division 72
  63rd (Royal Naval) Division 79
  1st Camerons Memorial 181
  Glasgow Highlanders 180
  Liverpool Pals Memorial 146
  Manchester Pals Memorial 137
  Marsden-Smedley Memorial 209-211
  Pozieres Memorial 114-114
  Salford Pals Memorial 102
  Tank Corps Memorial 111
  Thiepval Memorial 15, 31, 32, 35, 75, 89, 90, 92-96, 102, 107, 160, 179
  Tomasin Memorial 132
  Villers-Bretonneux Memorial 107
  Wallace Memorial 178
Montauban 133, 139-148, 163-164, 168, 181
Munro, H.H.('Saki') 95

Nab Valley 89, 91
Neville, Billie 141
Newfoundland Park 31, 50, 67-73, 77, 79, 80, 81, 82, 101, 160, 161

OG1 104, 107, 114

OG2 104, 107
Old Beaumont Road 46, 49-50, 58, 61
Ovillers 87, 89, 103, 104, 105, 113, 115

Parker, Ernest 192-193
Plowman, Max 137
Pope's Nose 81, 101
Pozieres 95, 103-115, 172
Pozieres Windmill 106, 107, 108, 110, 112, 202
Prowse, C.B. Brig-Gen 35-36, 160

Quadrilateral 35
Quarry Post 86, 89

Redan Ridge 29, 31, 32, 61, 63, 66, 151, 153, 154
Richards, Frank 177
Rossignol Wood 21-22
Roper, R.G. Mjr 124-125

'Saki' 95
St Pierre Divion 80, 101
Sassoon, Siegfried 127, 129-131, 132-133, 137
Schwaben Redoubt 100, 160
Serre 29-45, 94, 129, 154
Sheffield Memorial Park 38-40
Shepherd, Ernest 191-192
Sunken Lane 54, 62-63, 66, 67
Switch Line/Trench 176, 179, 187

Talus Boise 142-143, 145, 147-148
Tambour Craters 121, 122-123
Tanks 80, 179, 184-193
Thiepval 75, 81, 83-102, 160, 161
Thiepval Wood 80, 81, 96, 100, 101
Thomas, David 2/Lt 129-130
Touvent Farm 37, 41, 43, 44-45
Trones Wood 96, 203-204, 206

Ulster Tower 80-81, 100-101

Victoria Cross Winners,
  Bradford, R.B. Lt-Col 199-200
  Cunningham, J. Pte 42-43
  Cooke, T. Pte 106-107, 114
  Cherry, P. Lt 110
  Castleton, C.C. Sgt 114
  Campbell, J.V. Lt-Col 186-187
  Chavasse, N.G. Capt 205-206
  Freyberg, B.C. Lt-Col 78
  Gill, A. Sgt 172
  Green, J.L. Capt 26-27
  Hardy, Rev. T. 21
  Jacka, A. Capt 107-109
  Loudoun-Shand, S.W. Mjr 117, 118, 120
  Travers, R. Sgt 21
  Turnbull, J.Y. Sgt 91-92

Waterhouse, Gilbert Lt 32-34
Waterlot Farm 211
White City 53-54, 62, 63, 65-66
Williamson, Henry 75
Wood Lane 172-173, 182

Y Ravine 70, 72-73, 75

# MUSÉE DES ABRIS - ALBERT

Underground museum below the Basilica in Albert. Fine collection of uniforms and equipment displayed on mannequins in cases representing dugout scenes, trenches, mining operations etc. Short video about the Somme battlefields. Many illustrations and maps. Souvenir and bookshop, selling safe battlefield artefacts. French Francs only accepted.

# HISTORIAL OF THE GREAT WAR - PÉRONNE

Modern museum, set out like an art gallery. Short on artefacts, the museum follows the history of the war largely through video screens, art and contemporary posters. Occasional exhibitions, lectures and meetings. There is a library for visitors- appointment necessary. Bookshop takes payment in French Francs only, but credit cards accepted. Refreshments in cafe within the museum.

# SOUTH AFRICAN MUSEUM DELVILLE WOOD

Devoted entirely to the history of the South African forces in twentieth century conflicts, much of the collection relates to the Great War. Superb bronzes chronicle the story, and it is worth a visit for these alone. Visitors' centre in the car parking area has good toilets, small cafe and bookshop selling an extensive range of books in English, militaria and safe battlefield souvenirs, postcards, stamps etc. English and French currency accepted. Varying opening times in the winter months: otherwise open Tuesdays to Sundays.

# ULSTER TOWER THIEPVAL

Small display of items relating to the history of the Irish regiments in the Great War. Filmshow describes the fighting at Thiepval on 1st July. Good toilets. Snacks for sale, with small selection of books and maps. French Francs only accepted. Closed Sundays and Mondays.